Manifest Anything You Can Imagine

MANIFEST ANYTHING

You Can Imagine

HOW TO USE THE LAW OF ATTRACTION TO ACHIEVE THE HEALTH, WEALTH, AND HAPPINESS OF YOUR DREAMS

P.J. "Papi" DiNuzzo, MBA, MSTx

MINDSET COACH

NEW YORK

LONDON • NASHVILLE • MELBOURNE • VANCOUVER

Manifest Anything You Can Imagine

How to Use the Law of Attraction to Achieve the Health, Wealth, and Happiness of Your Dreams

Published in New York, New York, by Morgan James Publishing. Morgan James is a trademark of Morgan James, LLC. www.MorganJamesPublishing.com

Proudly distributed by Publishers Group West®

ISBN 9781636982960 paperback
ISBN 9781636982977 ebook
Library of Congress Control Number:
2023944115

Morgan James is a proud partner of Habitat for Humanity Peninsula and Greater Williamsburg. Partners in building since 2006.

Get involved today! Visit: www.morgan-james-publishing.com/giving-back

This Book Is Dedicated to:
Pasquale (Patsy) and Rose
Joe (Pappap) and Anna
Natale (Ned) and Phyllis
Nick and Renee
Mike, Jessica, and Estelle
Patsy, Michaela, Lucca, Pasquale, and Rocco
Renee, Avery, Danica, and Allison
Mark and Jackie
Thank you for your faith, family, hard work, loyalty, authenticity,
genuineness, gratitude, appreciation, heritage, tradition, legacy, guidance,
wisdom, time, patience, passion, understanding, support, and listening.
If you weren't you, I could never be me.
I love all of you and am forever IN Gratitude™ for the immeasurable gifts
you have provided me during my life.

Contents

Read This First:
Why I Wrote My Book

"The Spirit in me greets the Spirit in you. My message is one of hope, inspiration, guidance, and peace of mind."
—P. J. DiNuzzo

My "Why."

If you have never met me, it might surprise you to see my name on the cover of this book.

In my line of work, most people wouldn't expect me to dedicate so much effort and resources to writing a self-improvement book. I help successful individuals, couples, partners, entrepreneurs, wealthy families, and very successful closely held private business owners achieve their business, financial, personal, lifestyle, and other important goals.

But if you've known me for a period of time, you would be surprised that I hadn't written this book *sooner*.

It's been said that each person experiences an event or two during their life that fundamentally changes them from that moment forward.

Like you, I've experienced several life-defining moments in my life. Each of them has stuck with me to this day.

Three of those moments—three seemingly simple interactions with the three most important women in my life, both of my grandmothers and my mom—fueled me to write the book you're holding in your hands right now.

They are also the reason I created additional guidance tools and resources related to the messages in my book.

And they're the reason my entire life's purpose has become to provide "Peace of Mind" and "Inspiration" to my fellow brothers and sisters, especially women and children in need, and *most especially* women and children of color who are in need.

It all started with a simple conversation with my Italian Grandma Rose...

Italian Grandma Rose...

Decades ago, starting when I was two years old, I developed a reputation for asking questions, a lot of them. There were even babysitters who returned me in the middle of babysitting to my house and my mom saying they couldn't take any more of me because I asked too many questions.

Most of those questions were insignificant. But nearly six decades ago, the way Grandma Rose answered two of them has stuck with me to this day.

I was approximately six years old, alone in the kitchen of my Italian grandma, Rose's, tiny apartment in Midland, Pennsylvania. Grandma Rose had come by boat from Naples, Italy, to the United States, landing in New York City.

When we think of Naples today, we think of beautiful beaches, historical sites, and delicious food. When she lived in Naples, however, it was known worldwide as a "slum." And when I say, slum, I mean *slum*. In fact, if you looked back over the last two hundred years to find the poster child for slums on planet earth, where she lived in Naples, unfortunately, would be very high on the list.

She stood five feet tall with shoes on, had thirteen children, and was married to my grandfather, Pasquale, or "Patsy," her entire adult life. She had met my grandfather here, in the steel mill town of Midland, Pennsylvania. He was from the same area in Naples, but they didn't know each other there.

Curious about her childhood, I asked her what her experience was like growing up in Naples. To my surprise, she told me she had only the equivalent of an elementary grade-school education.

As a young kid in the 1960s, I wondered how someone born and raised in Italy with only a third-grade education could end up in the United States in the first place, never mind in a small steel mill town outside of Pittsburgh, Pennsylvania.

How did she get here without losing her Life or coming close to it? I wondered.

So I asked.

Grandma Rose told me she left Italy with only a piece of paper in her hand. Written on the paper was only a name and an address. She was told to go to the address, in Midland, Pennsylvania, where she would find people from her village in Italy who could help her.

But why did she leave Italy?

"I could no swingadaham," she told me with her thick Italian accent, for she spoke very little English.

What?

"I could no swingadaham," she repeated

After a few moments, I realized that because of her small size, she meant that she couldn't "swing a hammer" anymore—*a huge sledgeham-mer*, that is.

With her lack of education, she explained, the only job she could find back in Italy involved swinging a sledgehammer at the stone quarries all day long, essentially turning big rocks into little ones. She tried for a while, in vain, to "swingadaham" until she said she would pass out. But eventually she just couldn't physically do it anymore.

Although the thought of this tiny, thin woman swinging a sledge-hammer all day was shocking and took my breath away, what stuck with me from the story wasn't the story itself *but the look in her eyes* as she told me.

I will never forget the look of despair in her eyes as she shared with me, both of us all alone in her apartment, what could cause her to leave everything and everyone she knew and loved to move to a strange land with nothing more than a piece of paper with a name and address. *She looked as if she saw death in that moment.* She was obviously trying to tell me a story about not being able to "swingadaham" in a matter-of-fact way that a young kid could understand. *But her eyes told a different story, one of anguish, desperation, and the belief that she had no choice, no options.*

She would either leave everything and everyone she knew and loved behind or she would face a short life and die.

I lost my innocence that day. Grandma Rose was no longer *just* a grandma to me. She became my first inspiration, my first muse, *my first hero.* I didn't know exactly what I would do, but even at such a young age, I swore to myself that I would do everything possible in my life to never see that look in her eyes, someone's eyes I was related to, or anyone else's eyes, ever again if there was anything I could do about it.

Polish Grandma Anna...

Like my Italian Grandma Rose, my Polish Grandma Anna's family was from one of the poorest places in the world, in her case, the ghettos outside of Warsaw, Poland.

Like Naples, Italy, when Grandma Rose lived there, the ghettos in Poland at that time would be similarly ranked as one of (if not *the*) worst ghettos on the face of the earth.

Grandma Anna's family also took a huge risk as well and traveled by boat to New York City and eventually settled in South Wheeling, West Virginia, where a lot of Polish people had immigrated. One evening, when she and her two sisters were all under the age of ten, her father was thrown in jail for the night with a few other gentlemen after a night of drinking during the time of prohibition in the United States.

The next morning, when the police went to get him from the cell, he was unresponsive. Dead. Although no "official" information was released, the facts were that the police threw him into the cell, and did so too hard, causing him to hit his head on the back of the wall and die.

The police admitted that his death was a result of their wrongdoing and offered my great-grandmother, Grandma Anna's mom, a deal. Because my great-grandfather was the sole wage earner and his death left her alone with three daughters and no money, the police said they would allow her to run a speakeasy to sell alcohol during the prohibition period and that they would look the other way. She was uncomfortable about it because of her shy personality, but she grudgingly accepted because she had no other way to pay her bills.

A couple of years later, my great-grandmother remarried; however, her new relationship was far from a happy ending. The man she ended up marrying was very insensitive and brutal to her and the girls.

For example, his rule in their house was that nobody could start to eat until he was done eating and that everyone had to be seated at the dinner table. Every evening, they watched in anxious anticipation for him to finish his dinner, hoping that he would leave some food so that my great-grandmother and the three girls could eat what, if anything, was left over. He didn't go without either. There were times when my great-grandmother would cook four pork chops and he would eat all four, leaving nothing to eat for Grandma Anna and her two sisters and mother. There were many days when she didn't eat anything, Grandma Anna told me.

When my Polish Grandma Anna first told me these things, I was a couple of years older than I had been in my Italian Grandma Rose's kitchen, but the look in her eyes brought me right back into that apartment kitchen a couple of years prior. *Grandma Anna had the same sadness, emptiness, and look of despair in her eyes* that Grandma Rose had when she told me about how she had come to the United States to avoid dying in the stone quarries of Italy.

With food, clothing, and shelter being so core to our physical, mental, and emotional well-being, Grandma Anna's constant fear that her stepfather would be the only one eating that day resulted in a lifetime of anxiety, fear, sorrow, and dejection.

That look in her eyes. There it was again. The one I promised myself I would work tirelessly to eliminate. I still didn't know how I could eliminate it. But I could not get that look out of my head, and I will never forget it.

My Mom, Phyllis

My mom, Phyllis, was the eldest of three children, borne by my Polish Grandma Anna. Being the only daughter and in the period of time she grew up, my mother spent her entire childhood, as a woman, "waiting her turn" or coming "second (or even third) fiddle" to her brothers and others.

However, in spite of her challenges, she was one of the strongest people I've ever known. My mother endured, raising two well-adjusted and successful children, achieving a storied career as an owner of various family-owned businesses, and leaving a legacy that has impacted thousands of people in Beaver County, Pennsylvania, and beyond.

Unlike her career and achievements, her childhood was far from storied, as she was often forced or guilted into taking on far more than any child or young adult should be required to take on.

My mom was an independent and hardworking woman, born and raised in the United States in another famous steel mill town, Aliquippa, Pennsylvania. You might wonder where she learned how to run businesses and assume she must have attended some prestigious boarding or private school followed by earning a four-year university degree, but she was given no such advantage. Quite the opposite.

First, before entering high school, her parents sat down with her and her brothers and told them they had enough money to send only one child to private high school, and it would not be her. My uncle, her brother, the middle child, was the one. He was tall, good-looking, athletic, and intelligent. He was the "golden child," so to speak, so he would be the only one to attend private high school and not her. She was going to Aliquippa public school instead.

Then, when Mom graduated from high school, the family had a similar conversation about college. "Pappap," what we affectionately called my grandfather, worked for over forty years in the Aliquippa Works steel mill, owned by Jones & Laughlin Steel Company and barely scraped by to make ends meet for a family of five. They only could afford to send one child to college. Again, my uncle would be the one. My mom and her other brother were told they would need to join the workforce and find work right after graduation and start paying their own way. So that's what my mom did.

After graduating from high school, she worked several office jobs, including at the Aliquippa Works steel mill, with the bank, and the Steel Mill Railroad before going into business with my dad Natale, "Ned." Always wise beyond her years, Mom saved and lived below her means while working her various jobs and began to enjoy some financial independence because of it.

All the while, the "golden child" graduated from high school and attended college a few hours away.

Again, her parents sat her down for yet another talk. She was already out of high school, becoming established in her career, paying her own way, and saving for her future. What else could they possibly want?

It was the "golden child" again. Being in college a few hours away from home was causing them and her brother problems. Her mom and dad wanted him to be able to get home more frequently and be able to get around near his college. But he didn't have a car.

But guess who did? That's right. My mom. And her parents asked her to *give* her car to her brother. Not their car. Her car. The one she'd saved up for and purchased and paid off the car loan for with her own money. All with the money she saved from the jobs she worked because her parents sent the "golden child," and not her, to private high school and college.

Of course, my mom, being such a kind, generous, and all-around amazing person, agreed.

My mom told me these stories of her trials and tribulations growing up across several conversations when I was young. *Each time, though, there was that look in my mom's eyes.* It wasn't as desperate or "life or death" as what Grandma Rose and Grandma Anna experienced, *but there was an emptiness, despair, and hopelessness in her eyes* that brought me right back to Grandma Rose's kitchen all over again.

Again, I swore to myself that I would dedicate my life to ridding the world of these emotions, helplessness, and looks, especially in women, children, and others in need. I wanted no child or grandchild to have to see that same look in their parents' or grandparents' eyes. And I wanted no human being to experience the same pain and absolute lack of hope that my mom and two grandmothers experienced.

And that's what I've dedicated my entire adult life to doing in my Tax and Wealth Management, Family Office, Real Estate, and Mindset Coaching careers and by sharing this and other messages with as many people as possible.

Over the years, I studied everything I could about mindset, success, personal growth and improvement, and how people could avoid feeling like (1) they had no choice but to die or leave everything and everyone they loved, like Grandma Rose, (2) they didn't know when they would eat their next meal or whether their basic needs could be met, like Grandma

Anna, or (3) they were not worthy or were stuck in "second class," like my mom, Phyllis.

In my journey, I came upon the "Secret" to Achieving all of those things, and more, a number of years ago, and I have been sharing that secret with as many people as I can in my personal and professional life. Unfortunately, I didn't discover the secret in time for me to share it with my grandmothers, but I *was* able to share it with my mom.

But sharing the secret with my mom and others in my family wasn't enough. The more I learned, the more committed I became to sharing the secret with as many of my fellow brothers and sisters as possible with the hope that other children, parents, and grandparents, and people just like you, would never have to experience the feelings behind those eyes or see that look on their loved ones' faces ever again.

This is my Calling.

This is my Passion.

This is my Purpose.

And this is why you're reading my book right now.

My Life's Purpose... My Why

There's an old saying attributed to Mark Twain that says, "The two most important days in your life are the day you are born and the day you find out why."

One of the primary and key elements in your process to *Manifest Anything You Can Imagine* that you want in life—which I help you with throughout my book—is understanding your Purpose, your "why," the reason you do anything you do.

Defining your purpose—your why—often will be the last thing you will figure out on your journey as you learn how to *Manifest Anything You Can Imagine*. It will often take you a while to be comfortable that you got it correct. That's completely natural. Although you and I are not talking about the "meaning of life," we *are* talking about the "meaning of *your* life." And we are so frequently trained to think too small, consider ourselves too weak, not good enough, unworthy, or "second fiddle." But I'm here to tell you that you—yes, *you*—are the opposite of each of those undesirable adjectives. You *are* strong enough to achieve big things—even bigger than you dream imaginable. You *are* good enough. You *are* worthy. And you are not second fiddle to anyone on planet earth. Your Spiritual Spark, Spiritual DNA, and Spirit are perfect.

Accepting these truths and taking control over your Subconscious Mind's "Paradigm" can take time, however. I recognize that. And that's another reason it can be challenging to identify a why to your liking when you begin to learn how to Manifest. It's the reason your why will likely adjust over time, as you get more comfortable working with the "secret" and Manifesting incredible things for you and those you love.

In my case, although my conversations with my mom and Grandma Anna confirmed that I was on the right track, I knew exactly why I was born the moment I saw the look in Grandma Rose's eyes as she shared how and why she came to the United States.

Since that day, although I haven't always articulated it in exactly the same way, which might not surprise you since I was barely in elementary school at the time, I knew my purpose in life.

My purpose—my why—is to deliver "peace of mind" and "inspiration" to my fellow brothers and sisters, especially women and children in need, and most especially women and children of color who are in need, through food, clothing, shelter, healthcare, transportation, education, and, most importantly, Spirituality and Faith. I deliver this peace of mind and inspiration to my fellow brothers and sisters, especially women and children in need, and most especially women and children of color who are in need through my biological family, my team family, my family of clients, my community family, and my Spiritual family... each and every one of my fellow brothers and sisters.

That's why I AM on earth.

That's why I AM here.

If you don't yet know why you're here, I want to help you find out.

My book will help you do exactly that.

Standing on the Shoulders of Giants

There is a famous quote that states, "If I have seen further, it is by standing on the shoulders of giants," which has been attributed to Sir Isaac Newton and become famous for the proposition that your understanding and achievements in life are in large part thanks to the efforts, understandings, and achievements of people who preceded you.

I feel that this quote is important because my book that you are holding in your hands right now is indeed the product of me standing on the shoulders of many giants.

For example, the most famous book about Manifesting is probably *Think and Grow Rich* by Napoleon Hill, which has sold more than *one hundred million* copies. Hill was not the first nor was he the last author to write on such an important topic.

In my mind, however, there's no giant on whose shoulders I stand taller than Wallace Wattles, who lived from the mid-1800s until February 7, 1911. His most famous book, *The Science of Getting Rich*, came out less than one year before his death. In it, Wattles identified the steps to being able to *Manifest Anything* you want in life, with a focus on explaining to people how to enjoy success, become wealthy, and achieve their goals.

What I loved about Wattles' book was that it was accurate, brief, and to the point. His book gave the basic building blocks, the addition and subtraction, the "how to," of Manifesting and creating your dream life more succinctly than any of the hundreds of other books I have read on the topic.

However, published in 1910, it might not surprise you that a significant amount of his text is outdated—not the addition and subtraction, the *how to*: steps are steps, math is math. You can't *improve* on math. One plus one has always equaled and will always equal two. But the references and ancillary material in his book are a bit dated—and I say that in love, with no negativity or criticism at all. In fact, when I thought about writing my book that you're holding, I thought that there was *no better* place for me to start than by using the core message of Wallace Wattles himself.

So that's what I did. I started with *The Science of Getting Rich*— which has long been in the public domain and free of copyright[1]—and then completely revamped, expanded, and modernized it to help you, today. Most of my updating, revamping, and additions are important and extensive, and only a distinct minority of his original words do remain. The math. The math that helped me Manifest so much good in my life.

What made *The Science of Getting Rich* so good, in my opinion, was how simple and short it was. It was the simplest and briefest book out of more than one hundred books I have read about the core of Manifesting and achieving your Best-Life. And its core message—the math—survives the test of time. I have researched and read extensively on the topic, and, like I mentioned above, there's no giant on whose shoulders I stand taller or owe more credit to than Wallace Wattles.

My goal is to *provide hope*, lead, guide, educate, and inspire you, and there was no better place to start. In many ways, this book, therefore, acts almost like the next iteration of the concepts in *The Science of Getting Rich*, taking the ball and moving it forward where Wallace Wattles left off more than one hundred years ago.

Although just a distinct minority of the words you're about to read come straight from Wallace Wattles himself, the bulk of my book is new

---

1   If you want to get a free digital copy of the complete original text of *The Science of Getting Rich*, you can download one at PJMindsetCoachInstitute.com.

content that I have generated, which adds to the concepts from his book and the knowledge I have gained over my lifetime of success so that you can truly build the life of your dreams no matter what your current situation looks like.

The Glossary and Concepts to Live By

As you'll see, many terms I use in my book have very specific meanings in the context of Manifesting your best future.

Some of them are new words altogether, words you may have never heard before. Others are words—or combinations of words—that have common understandings but are used differently in this context.

For these reasons, I also included a glossary of terms at the end of this book.

I suggest looking through the glossary and concepts to live by *before* you begin to read my book so you can familiarize yourself with many of the new concepts you are about to encounter.

Once you start reading my book, I believe you will also find it helpful to regularly flip back and forth between the content and glossary for better understanding.

The Secret

Finally, I highly recommend watching the movie *The Secret*, a 90-minute documentary by Rhonda Byrne released in 2006, *before* you read the rest of my book.[2]

The Secret, which is a feature film adaptation of Rhonda Byrne's best-selling book by the same name, will give you tremendous insight into the potential impact to *Manifest Anything You Can Imagine* and the information you're about to read can have on your life.

---

2   You can find links to several places where you can access the movie on PJMindsetCoachInstitute.com.

It can show you how to use Universal Intelligence and the other information you're about to read to Manifest and achieve peace of mind, inspiration, and anything else you want in life. Unfortunately, Grandma Rose, Grandma Anna, and my mom, Phyllis, never knew this secret when they needed it, although I was able to share some of it with my mother in her later years.

You will come to know that these truths can help you achieve anything you want no matter where you live, your personal background, gender, age, financial background, or any other circumstance you currently find yourself in today.

They don't cost a penny.

They don't require a degree.

You don't need experience.

Or expertise.

Or any other qualification to use them.

You have everything you need already inside you.

You have Universal Intelligence and the Universal Subconscious Mind on your side.

You have all the Universal Laws on your side.

Your Spiritual Spark, Spiritual DNA, and Spirit are perfect.

The (Social) Proof Is in the Pudding

The book you hold in your hands has the power to change your life. How do I know? Because I used the same information to change mine (and millions of other people have too).

My father died when I was in my early twenties and left my mom, my brother, Mark, and me with the equivalent of $2 million in debt, in today's dollars. Some kind of "inheritance," huh?

Plain and simple, I started out life in a hole, a *big* hole. It took us fifteen years of working six to seven days per week at the family restaurant to pay it down so we could finally start our lives and move on.

After this experience, and vowing to never go through anything like that again, I have built my entire life based on the principles you will learn over the rest of my book. Other millionaires have too.

I went...

- **from** $2 million in debt...
- **to** total business revenue (sales) now approaching $10 million per year.
- **from** my first client hiring me to manage just $2,000...
- **to** my current household minimum account size of $2 million.
- **from** managing zero accounts...
- **to** now managing more than 2,500 accounts.
- **from** managing $0...
- **to** approaching $1 billion in Assets Under Management.
- **from** zero books written...
- **to** having written half a dozen books and hitting numerous national and international bestseller lists including the *Wall Street Journal* and *USA Today* and having the #1 bestselling non-fiction book on all of Amazon and the #1 bestselling book on all of Barnes and Noble's website.
- **from** owning $0 in real estate...
- **to** building a multimillion-dollar real estate portfolio.

Starting from zero dollars, I built a Family Office, serving clients with $25 million to $250+ million of Net Worth, and a Tax and Wealth Management Firm managing approximately $1 billion. We've served individuals, couples, families, entrepreneurs, and successful closely held private businesses in thirty-plus states around the US without merging with another firm, buying another firm, or bringing in an outside partner who had accounts already under management. Just 100 percent natural, internally generated, organic growth!

The Universal Way principles I share with you took me from $0 to nearly $1 billion!

Financial Advisor magazine recently ranked my firm in the top four hundred out of more than twenty thousand firms in the US.

I have a very successful Real Estate Company.

I have a very successful Self-Improvement Mindset Coaching Company.

And all I did to Manifest this was use the same principles you will learn over the rest of my book.

I also used these principles to Manifest success far beyond my Family Office, Tax and Wealth Management firm, P. J. MindsetCoach Company, and Real Estate Company.

For example, I used them to write half a dozen books, with more on the way. I used them to Manifest hitting the *Wall Street Journal Top 5* bestseller's list. I used them to Manifest hitting the *USA Today* bestseller list. I used them to Manifest having the #1 nonfiction book on all of Amazon. I used them to Manifest having the #1 overall book on Barnes & Noble's website, and much, much more.

I know these principles work because I've used them myself to *Manifest Anything You Can Imagine*.

And I Want the same for you.

I Want you to Manifest whatever level of success *you* want.

I Want you to Manifest *your* dream life.

I Want you to change your family tree for generations to come.

But, to be clear, this is not a "do as I say, not as I do" book.

This is a "do as I *actually did*" book.

It's a "do as thousands of other people and millionaires have done" book.

I built my book as an improved way to Manifest the ideas shared in *Think and Grow Rich*, Napoleon Hill's self-improvement book that has sold over one hundred million copies.

I built my book as an improved way to Manifest the ideas shared in the 2006 hit documentary movie *The Secret*.

My book is a book that shares time-tested principles that many people have used to *Manifest Anything You Can Imagine*.

The only question left is, will you be next?

If you take action and consistently follow the principles I have used and share over the rest of my book, I'm confident your answer to that question will be "Yes."

For the rest of my book, I'm going to show you exactly how to Manifest and live your best, most abundant life possible.

And the look I saw in my grandmothers' and mother's eyes will never appear in *your* eyes.

Join me.

Foreword by Keshia Rush

ot too long ago, I was just like many of you. My husband, Tray, and I were working jobs we didn't like, barely scraping by, and most desperately dreamed of a better life.

We tried everything to break out—from small business ideas to network marketing to getting new jobs—but nothing seemed to help us get ahead. You name a side hustle or business opportunity and we probably tried it.

But nothing seemed to work; that is, until we discovered we had everything we needed to achieve our dreams right inside ourselves. Yet I looked at people around me, driving nice cars, living in big houses, and wearing nice clothes. Although I wasn't motivated by material things like that, my financial situation at the time was so tight that I couldn't even think about luxuries like those. Seeing people in my neighborhood enjoying those luxuries suggested to me that it was possible for me too. I just hadn't yet figured out how to achieve a level of success beyond living paycheck to paycheck.

Eventually, I discovered that the future my husband and I dreamed of *was* possible, but only if we stopped looking initially to outside solutions and started looking right inside ourselves, to Manifesting our dream life and getting opportunities to come to us.

We searched within ourselves, and the opportunities of our dreams were attracted to and found us.

Although it wasn't always smooth sailing as we faced many obstacles along the way, within a few short years, we were able to Manifest our dream life.

In our world, that dream life looks like hosting a thriving YouTube community with well over ten million subscribers and generating more than four billion views, owning our dream home, driving our dream cars, and building additional dream businesses to build a legacy to support our family and the world around us for generations to come.

I have had the opportunity to work with some incredible people, including helping Justin Trudeau, the Prime Minister of Canada, perform his first YouTube live stream several years ago.

I have also become a published children's book author, writing children's books to help families facilitate important conversations at home. My first two children's books, each with a companion coloring book, are already in production as I write this short message to you, and I've begun writing the next books in the series as well.

If you had met me years ago, however, you might never have guessed that I'd be living the life I am living now. And you wouldn't have been alone in that thinking. People in my family even worried about me.

First, nobody in my family has achieved anything remotely close to what I've been able to Manifest in my life, especially at such a young age. When I think of my family, they're incredible people, but they're not financially free; they work jobs they don't love, and they don't live lives by design. So nobody expected my life to be any different.

Nobody except me and my husband, that is.

My success didn't stop with me either. The same people who worried about me for wanting more in life eventually asked me how I did it as they observed me achieving greater and greater levels of Success.

Even better, I'm now able to help my family, too, and inspire them to take action to Manifest greater things for themselves as well. And I've been able to show my kids that work doesn't need to be boring and that they can achieve extraordinary levels of wealth, health, and happiness.

And I did it all by using the same exact principles and processes my friend and trusted advisor P. J. DiNuzzo will share with you over the rest of his book. I have gotten to know P. J. and have spent a lot of time with him. I know what is in his heart to help share these secrets with the world to help his fellow brothers and sisters, particularly women and children, and especially women and children of color Manifest opportunities that many of them never would think are possible. And I know what he teaches works because it's worked for me and I've seen it work for other people just like you and me.

I don't say any of this to brag but to show you what's possible if you apply what you're about to read from P. J., every day, for the rest of your life.

The truth is, I know in my heart that none of what I've achieved would have been possible if I had not stopped searching for the next side hustle or business opportunity and started Manifesting the future I wanted for myself and my family.

The book you hold in your hands could do the same for you if you take action. It's full of the real keys to Manifesting your dream life. But it won't help you if you don't keep going, keep reading, and then take action on the timeless truths you're about to read.

As a wife, mother, and woman of color, I appreciate P. J.'s dedication to supporting his fellow brothers and sisters, especially women and children, and, most especially, women and children of color who are in need.

For someone in P. J.'s position, who helps some of the wealthiest people manage their family, finances, businesses, and future goals, the "easy" route for him would be to create this content and sell it to those who could pay the most money. After all, just one more client for his DiNuzzo Family Office could yield him more money than selling thousands upon thousands of books. Or he could focus on his real estate company and add hundreds of thousands of dollars a year in rental income. His other successful businesses could add millions of dollars to his net worth. The easiest thing for P. J. to do would be to focus on his finance businesses.

But that's not who P. J. is. And that's exactly why you're reading this book right now. In the time I've gotten to know P. J., I have grown to both trust and admire him. What he does for his clients is far beyond what most people in his business do. And what he's built for himself, going from managing $0 to nearly $1 billion completely organically is unheard of.

Unlike many people in his shoes, P. J. cares more about sharing these secrets with regular people just like you instead of adding even millions of dollars to his bank account. So he's sharing information with you and other people like you who may never hire him to put together a sophisticated financial, family, business, or other plan for their future—that is, not until they (you!) take action like I did and Manifest the life of *your* dreams just like I Manifested mine.

Inspired by the three most important and pivotal women in his life, his two grandmothers and his mom, who each came from humble means, P. J.'s focus is to reach those who *need* this content the most, irrespective of whether they have an ability to pay *anything* to him anytime soon.

In fact, if you know someone who can't afford to buy this book, P. J. has generously set up a website where anyone can download a free digital copy. Just visit ManifestAnythingFree.com and let him know where to send it.

—Keshia Rush

Preface

"I have in my Subconscious Mind what I believe is the greatest gift on earth and I call it 'P. J.'s Magic Lamp.' I believe you have your own 'Magic Lamp' in your Subconscious Mind as well and it is my purpose on earth to guide you in how to use it to Manifest successfully. Aladdin's Magic Lamp only granted him three wishes, while P. J.'s Magic Lamp (and yours) are granted unlimited wishes by Universal Intelligence. There is one catch, though. Because the Universe was created and lives in balance and harmony, the Magic Lamps the Universe entrusted in us are programmed to take action on both positive and negative suggestions from ourselves, others, or any other source. Learn how to use your Magic Lamp to Manifest Anything You Can Imagine and guard it with your life."
—P. J. DiNuzzo

Namaste...
The Spirit in me greets the Spirit in *you*.
Welcome, my friend.

I AM beyond excited about our journey together and guiding you to make the Law of Attraction work for you to *Manifest Anything You Can Imagine*.

But first, before we get started... you get to address your initial most important "fork in the road."

Grab a blank piece of paper and a pen and place them on the table in front of you.

In large letters down the left-hand side of the paper, write...

H

W

H

The top "H" is for "Health." The "W" is for "Wealth." And the bottom "H" is for "Happiness."

To the right of each letter, give yourself a grade like you would in school (A, B, C, D, or F) as to how successful you have been and currently are regarding each of these three key areas in living your Best-Life.

If you give yourself an "A" grade, or close to it, for all three areas, Health, Wealth, and Happiness, my book is *not* for you.

If your grades are less than you desire, and it seems that nothing you do or have done in the past has been able to help... you were guided to the right place.

I created my book especially for you.

Imagine you and I sitting in your favorite coffee shop with the aroma of your favorite beverage in the air, the two of us sitting off to the side in the two most comfortable seats in the place, having the greatest one-on-one conversation of your life. Our conversation is all about you and your success, happiness, and living your Best-Life.

I wrote my book to and for you as a reflection of that initial and personal ongoing conversation between you and me.

Ideally, read my book right before you fall asleep at night or first thing in the morning, immediately after you awaken.

For these are the times you are closest to Universal Intelligence and the Universal Subconscious Mind and the time that the knowledge you are acquiring will be most powerful, impactful, and beneficial for you.

Right now, as you start on your journey with me and throughout reading my book, which I crafted especially for you, it *does not* matter if you believe everything 100 percent or even close to it. All that matters is for you to know in your heart of hearts that I BELIEVE IN YOU 100 PERCENT!

My belief in you will *not* waiver.

My belief in you and that *you* can Manifest your Best-Life is 100 percent.

If you so choose to focus and use your all-powerful free will, we are beginning the most magnificent lifelong journey together.

As Neville Goddard stated, "The great secret is a controlled imagination and a well-sustained attention firmly and repeatedly focused on the feeling of the wish fulfilled until it fills the mind and crowds all other ideas out of consciousness."

My book is to be viewed and used as a practical manual, not as a debate tool regarding Universal Laws and theories. It is intended for all of my brothers and sisters, especially women and children in need, and most especially women and children of color who are in need. For most people in need, their most pressing need is for money, and for them, reaching a level of financial security and success means everything, for it can be beyond life-changing for them and their loved ones.

My book is for you, and my fellow brothers and sisters, who have, so far, not been satisfied regarding your pursuit of health, Spirit, happiness, wealth, love, or life itself.

I expect you to take my heartfelt statements regarding Universal Intelligence and the Universal Subconscious Mind upon Faith, just as you would take fundamental statements concerning the Law of Gravity, upon Faith, acting as if you absolutely believe them to be true and acting on them without fear, doubt, or hesitation.

I ask of you to listen to me and follow me until you find one of two things not to be true: 1) I do not know what I am talking about, or 2) I am lying.

You will not encounter or experience either option.

I am confident that every person who listens to and truly hears my guidance *with their heart* as directed from Universal Intelligence and takes action can certainly *Manifest Anything* You Can Imagine, for the Universal Intelligence Science I am teaching is an exact science that flows directly out of the Universal Laws and comes directly from the Source, and if followed properly, failure is impossible.

Universal Intelligence makes One Infinite Power available to each and every one of us.

Starting right now, I AM leading and guiding you to success beyond your wildest dreams from where you are today.

I will teach you, lead you, and guide you.

It feels so good inside that we are starting a lifelong success-filled journey together.

The fundamental theory of the Universe—the theory that One is All, and that All is One, that one Universal Intelligent Substance Manifests Itself as the seemingly many elements of the material world—should rightly be credited in my Mind as being rediscovered and emphasized by Hinduism, and one that has been gradually winding and winning its way into the thought of the western world for the last three hundred years.

Universal Intelligence is the foundation of most Asian philosophies, and those of Plato, William Shakespeare, Isaac Newton, Ludwig van Beethoven, James Allen, Abraham Lincoln, Ralph Waldo Emerson, Wallace Wattles, Thomas Troward, Andrew Carnegie, Thomas Edison, Albert Einstein, Napoleon Hill, Neville Goddard, U. S. Andersen, Earl Nightingale, and Bob Proctor.

The torch has been directly passed over the past 125+ years from Andrew Carnegie to Napoleon Hill to Earl Nightingale to Bob Proctor... And now... here I AM.

In writing my book, I have sacrificed all other considerations to plainness and simplicity of style, so that you can more easily understand. I am not here to impress. I am here to *provide hope*, lead, guide, educate, and inspire. Although the keys to _Manifest Anything You Can Imagine_ have been kept a virtual "secret" over the past two thousand-plus years, the plan of action I have laid out within my book has been deduced from the conclusions of Universal Intelligence. It has been proven over the history of humankind and bears the supreme test of practical experimentation; in plain English, *it works*. If you want to live your Best-Life, achieve your dreams and wishes, enjoy happiness, and succeed for yourself, your family, your relationships, and your loved ones, read my book, *and do exactly as I direct and instruct you to do.*

Big Picture...

All Original Creation is done...

Original Creation is complete and has been for eons...

As the Universe was Created eons and eons ago...

The Universal Laws founded at the inception of the Universe are Perfect, Precise, ongoing, and in place as we speak today.

When Created, and built upon Universal Laws, one of the foundational concepts the Universe was brought into existence under is "the Law of Perpetual Increase."

The Universe, as you will come to see and experience, is the most glorious "machine" ever built... Perfect... Infinite... Abundant... and "Programmed" for eternal Expression, Expansion, Increase, Growth, Manifesting, Wisdom, Love, Life, Abundance, Joy, Harmony, and Happiness.

You do *not* live in a zero-sum world; quite the contrary, you live in a "Thought World," within a Perfect and Infinite "Thought Universe," filled with *unlimited abundance.*

Nothing is Created or destroyed... All of the knowledge there ever has been or ever will be is already here.

Everything in the Universe is *energy*. Energy cannot be created or destroyed. It always was, always is, and forever will be. *Energy moves into form and through form and out of form over and over and over again.*

All of the *Power* that there ever has been or ever will be is already here.

Universal Power is 100 percent evenly present in you and in all places at all times.

It is within you right now.

Your Spiritual Spark, Spiritual DNA, and Spirit are Perfect.

I was directed to write my book to *provide hope*, lead, teach, guide, instruct, and inspire you about how to use your mind properly and Co-Create your Best-Life with Universal Intelligence.

Follow me and let me lead and show you how to hitch a ride, surf with the flow, and live in harmony on and with this astounding "Perpetual Increase Machine" to Manifest your dreams and wishes for your Health, Wealth, Spirit, Love, Relationships, Faith, Family, and Happiness.

"My hopes were high, and I looked every day for some change to take place. What it was to be I knew not, but that it would come I felt certain if I kept on.... One day the chance came."
—Andrew Carnegie

Chapter 1:

Your Right to Express, Expand, Increase, Grow, Success, Happiness, and... Manifest Anything

*"Wealth is not to feed our egos, but to feed the hungry
and to help people help themselves."*
—Andrew Carnegie

*"You control a lot by your thoughts, and we control a lot by our joined
thoughts . . . by what I (and we) believe. When I started to figure that
out for myself, I became careful of what I think and what I ask for. I
was like what else can I do? What else can I manifest, because I have
seen it work. I have seen it happen over and over again."*
—Oprah Winfrey

"I ask of you to listen to me and follow me until you find one of two things not to be true: (1) I do not know what I am talking about, or (2) I am lying. You will not encounter or experience either option. It does not matter at this time if you believe in yourself 100 percent or even close to it. All that matters is for you to know in your heart of hearts that I BELIEVE IN YOU 100 PERCENT."
—P. J. DiNuzzo

Whatever may be said in praise of poverty, the fact remains that it is not possible for you to live your real, absolute Best-Life unless you can enjoy success and happiness. I am here to teach you how. I define your "Best-Life" as success in living richly in Body, Mind, Spirit, Heart, Health, and Wealth. You cannot rise to your greatest possible height in health, wealth, happiness, or growth unless you have ample money, for to truly unfold your Spirit, to be in harmony with Universal Intelligence, and to develop your special talents, you must grow and have the use of many things, and you cannot have these things unless you have the money to buy them with.

The exciting news that I bring to you is that *Universal Intelligence has a Burning-Desire* for you to have and enjoy all of this... and more.

You develop and grow in mind, Spirit, heart, and body by making use of things, and the world is so organized that you must have the currency of exchange—money—in order to become the possessor of things; therefore, the basis of all advancement for you must be the Universal Science of living your Best-Life.

The object of the Universe and all of the life It Created is fuller development, expression, expansion, increase, growth, and happiness, and everything that lives has an inalienable right to happiness, according to Universal Intelligence and all the development it is capable of attaining.

Your free will and right to life mean your right to have the free and unrestricted use of all the things that may be necessary for your fullest mental, Spiritual, emotional, and physical unfoldment.

In my book, I shall not speak of success in a figurative way, for to really enjoy your Best-Life does not mean to be satisfied or content with a little. Universal Intelligence does not want you to be satisfied with a little if you are capable of using and enjoying more. The purpose of Universal Intelligence is the advancement and unfoldment of life, and accordingly, you should have all that can contribute to the power, elegance, beauty, and richness of your life. To be content with less would place you out of harmony with Universal Intelligence and the limitless gifts It has made available to you.

When you own all you want for the Living of all the life you are capable of living, you are experiencing your Best-Life, and if you have a lack of money, you cannot have all that you want. Life has advanced so far, and become so complex, that even the most ordinary man or woman requires a great amount of wealth in order to live in a manner that even approaches completeness. You and your Spirit naturally want to become all that you are capable of becoming. This desire for you to realize your unlimited innate possibilities is inherent in human nature, for you cannot help wanting to be all that you can be. Success in life is becoming what you want to be; you can become what you want to be only by making use of things, and you can have the free use of things only as you become successful enough to buy them.

When you are in alignment with Universal Intelligence, you never feel guilty, for you know that Universal Intelligence makes a million dollars with the same ease as it makes a carrot, or a leaf on a tree or bush, or a grain of sand.

To understand Universal Intelligence's Science of Success and Manifesting is therefore the most essential of all knowledge.

There is nothing wrong with you wanting to enjoy success and live your Best-Life; quite the opposite, it actually places you directly and completely in harmony with Universal Intelligence.

The desire to fully express, enjoy, expand, increase, grow, and Manifest is *not* greed, nor is it wrong. The desire to succeed is really the desire for a richer, fuller, and more abundant life, and that desire is praisewor-thy. If you did not desire to live more abundantly, it would be unusual, and so the person who does not desire to have money enough to buy all that they want is not in harmony with Universal Intelligence's desire for fuller expression, expansion, and growth.

There are four motives for which we live: we live for the body, we live for the mind, we live for the Spirit, and we live for the heart. No one of these is better than the other; all are equally desirable. And no one of the four—body, mind, Spirit, or heart—can live fully if any of the others are cut short of full life and expression. It is not right or noble to live only for the Spirit and deny mind and body as well as heart. It's also wrong to live for the mind and deny body, Spirit, and heart.

We are all acquainted with the loathsome consequences of living for the body and denying the mind, Spirit, and heart, and we see that real life means the complete expression of all that you can give forth through body, mind, heart, and Spirit. Whatever people may say, no one can be really happy and live their Best-Life unless their body is living fully in every function, and unless the same is true of their mind, heart, and Spirit. Wherever there is unexpressed possibility, or function not per-formed, there is unsatisfied desire.

Desire is possibility seeking expression.

Desire, a Burning-Desire *with full emotion*, is the Universe's magical power that brings your goal to you through your Subconscious Mind and its direct connection with Universal Intelligence.

You cannot live fully in body without good food, comfortable cloth-ing, warm shelter, or freedom from excessive toil. Rest, recreation, and travel are also necessary to your success and your rich physical life.

You cannot live fully and richly in mind without books and time to study them, without opportunity for travel and observation, or without intellectual companionship.

To live fully and richly in mind, you must have intellectual recreations, and you must surround yourself with all the objects of art and beauty you are capable of enjoying and appreciating.

To live fully and richly in Spirit, you must have love, and love is denied full expression by poverty.

Your highest happiness is found in the bestowal of benefits on those you love. Love finds its most natural and spontaneous expression in giving. It is in the use of material things that you find full life for your body, develop your mind, and unfold your Spirit. It is, therefore, of supreme importance to you to Manifest and enjoy your Best-Life.

It is perfectly right that you should desire to succeed and live your Best-Life. If you are a typical person, you cannot help doing so. For the Universe to be in harmony, it is the noblest and most necessary of all studies. If you neglect this study, you are failing in your duty as a Co-Creator with Universal Intelligence, and you're failing humanity, for you can render Universal Intelligence no greater service than to make the most of yourself and improve all those around you.

Chapter 2:

There Is a Universal Intelligence Science of Achieving Success and Happiness

"If you change the way you look at things, the things you look at change."
—Wayne Dyer

"Like attracts like. You have to understand, you are a magnet. Whatever you are, that's what you draw to you. If you're negative, you're going to draw negativity. You positive? You draw positive. You're a kind person? More people are kind to you... If you see it in your mind, you can hold it in your hand. This is so true."
—Steve Harvey

"The 'secret' that Andrew Carnegie described and detailed to Napoleon Hill in Hill's book, Think and Grow Rich, is the Law of Attraction."
—P. J. DiNuzzo

There are immutable Universal Laws to success, and it is an exact science, like algebra or arithmetic laid out eons ago in spellbinding accuracy and detail by Universal Intelligence. There are specific Universal Laws that govern the process of success and Manifesting, and once you learn and live your life guided by these Universal Laws, you will succeed and live richly with mathematical and absolute certainty.

Success in wealth, health, love, Spirit, and life come as a result of doing things in the Universal Way. Those who do things in the Universal Way, whether on purpose or accidentally, succeed, while those who do not do things in the Universal Way, no matter how hard they work or how able they are, remain poor and frustrated.

It is Universal Law and the Law of Attraction that *like causes always produce like effects,* and, therefore, any man or woman who learns to do things in the Universal Way will infallibly succeed.

The "secret" that Andrew Carnegie described and detailed to Napoleon Hill in Hill's book, *Think and Grow Rich*, is the Law of Attraction. Everything in your life has been attracted to you, by you, from the images you hold in your mind and thoughts.

If you can think the thought and create the thought-form in your mind you can hold it in your hand.

As a result, you become what you think about.

Success is not a matter of environment, for if it were, all the people in certain neighborhoods would become wealthy, the people of one city would all be successful, while those of other towns would all be poor, or the inhabitants of one state would roll in wealth, while those of an adjoining state would be in poverty.

However, everywhere you see rich and poor living side by side, in the same environment, and often engaged in the same vocations. When two people are in the same locality, and in the same business, and one gets rich while the other remains poor, it shows that success is not, primarily, a matter of environment. Some environments may be more favorable than others, but when two people in the same business are in the same neighborhood, and one succeeds while the other fails, it indicates that true success is the result of doing things in the Universal Way.

And further, the ability to do things in the Universal Way is not due solely to the possession of talent, for many people who have great talent remain poor, while others who have very little talent succeed.

In studying the people who have been successful, you will find that *they are an average lot in all respects*, having no greater talents and abilities than other people. It is evident that they do not Succeed because they possess talents and abilities that others do not, but because they happen to do things in the Universal Way.

Success is not the result of saving, or "thrifting"; many very frugal people are poor, while free spenders often succeed.

Nor is success due to doing things that others fail to do, for two people in the same business often do almost exactly the same things, and one succeeds while the other remains poor or becomes bankrupt.

As you will see, from all these things, you will come to the conclusion that success, Manifesting, and living your Best-Life are the result of doing things in the Universal Way.

If success is the result of doing things in the Universal Way, and if *through the Law of Attraction, like causes always produce like effects*, then if you can do things in that way, you can succeed, and the whole matter is brought within the domain and certainty of Universal Laws and exact science.

The question arises here of whether the Universal Way may be so difficult that only a few may be able to follow it. But this cannot be true, as you have seen, so far as natural ability is concerned. Talented people succeed, and nontalented people succeed. Intellectually brilliant people succeed, and nonintellectually brilliant people succeed. Physically strong people succeed, and physically weak and sickly people succeed.

Some degree of ability to think and understand is, of course, essential, but in so far as natural ability is concerned, any man or woman who has sense enough to read and understand my words can certainly succeed, Manifest, and live their Best-Life.

Also, you have seen that while it is not a matter of environment, location counts for something. You would not go to the heart of a vast desert and expect to do successful business.

Being successful and Manifesting your goal involves the necessity of dealing with men and women, and of being where there are people to deal with, and if these people are inclined to deal in the way you want to deal, so much the better. But that is about as far as environment goes.

If *anybody* else in your town can succeed, so can you, and if anybody else in your state can succeed, so can you, and if anybody else in your country can succeed, so can you.

If anyone on earth has ever accomplished a specific goal, then you know that you can too.

Again, it is not a matter of choosing some particular business or profession. People succeed in every business and in every profession, while their next-door neighbors in the same vocation remain in poverty.

It is true that you will do best in a business or profession you like, one that is congenial to you, and if you have certain talents that are well developed, you will do best in a business or profession that calls for the exercise of those talents.

Also, you will do best in a business that is suited to your locality. An ice-cream parlor would do better in a warm climate than at the North or South Pole. Winter coats will sell better in the North or South Pole than in a year-round warm climate.

But, aside from these obvious general limitations, your success is not dependent upon your engaging in some particular business, but upon your learning to do things in the Universal Way. If you are now in business, and anybody else in your locality is succeeding in the same business while you are *not*, it is because you are not doing things in the same way that the other person is doing them.

That is what I AM here for.

You are not prevented from succeeding or from being able to *Manifest Anything You Can Imagine* by lack of capital. True, as you get capital, the increase becomes more easy and rapid. No matter how poor you may be, if you begin to do things in the Universal Way, you will begin to Manifest what you want and succeed, and you will begin to have capital. The getting of capital is a part of the process of success, and it is a part of the result that will invariably follow and flow to you when you do things in the Universal Way.

You may be the poorest person on the continent and be deeply in debt, and you may have neither friends nor influence nor resources, but if you begin to do things as I proscribe in the Universal Way, you must infallibly Manifest your goal, for *like causes must produce like effects.*

You are a magnet and you attract toward you the exact type of energy that you put out into the Universe.

If you have no capital, you can get capital; if you are in the wrong business, you can get into the right business; if you are in the wrong location, you can go to the right location, and you can do so *by beginning in your present business and in your present location* to do things in the Universal Way, which causes success.

Chapter 3:

Is Your Opportunity to Manifest Success and Achieve Your Goal Monopolized?

"No matter what your present job, it has enormous possibilities
if you are willing to pay the price."
—Earl Nightingale

"If you can think the thought and create the thought-form
in your mind, with the emotion of that of a child on
Christmas morning, you can hold it in your hand."
—P. J. DiNuzzo

You are never kept poor because opportunity has been taken away from you, or because you think other people have monopolized the wealth and have put a fence around it. You may be shut off from engaging in business in certain lines, but there are *always* other channels open to you.

13

It is quite true that if you are an employee of a large organization that is insensitive to its employees, you have very little chance of becoming the owner of the organization in which you work, but it is also true that if you begin to act in the Universal Way, you can leave the employ of the organization and find success elsewhere.

In our world, at different evolutionary periods in time, the tide of opportunity sets in different directions, according to the needs of the whole and the particular stage of social evolution that has been reached.

There is an abundance of opportunity for you to go with the tide, instead of trying to swim against it. Always find the direction of the flow and ride it. Let It and Universal Intelligence do the work for you and Co-Create with them.

Factory employees, either as individuals or as a class, are not deprived of opportunity. The employees are not being "kept down" by their owners and supervisors; they are not being "ground into the dirt" by the leaders of industry. As a class, they are where they are because they are not using Universal Intelligence's tools that are available to them, and they are not doing things in the Universal Way.

Members of the working class may easily become the leadership class whenever they begin to do things in the Universal Way, for the Law of Wealth is the same for them as it is for all others. This they must learn or they will remain where they are for as long as they continue to do as they do. The individual employee, however, is not held down by the ignorance or the mental slothfulness of their class, for they can follow the tide of opportunity to success, and my book will teach them and you how.

No one is kept in poverty by a shortness in the supply of opportunity or abundance. There is more than enough for all. *There is no Scarcity; there can be and only is Abundance.* The visible supply is practically inexhaustible and the invisible supply really *is* inexhaustible.

Your mind can only be at one moment in time, *in the present*, in one of only four mindsets: CAFPA, which stands for, (1) Creative or Competitive, (2) Abundance or Scarcity, (3) Faith or Fear, and (4) Positive Attitude (High Vibration) or Negative Attitude (Low Vibration), on the "+" or "-" side of your mind. Always do everything you can to be in and remain in a Creative, Abundance, Faith, Positive Attitude/High Vibration, and a "+" Mindset. If you find yourself in a Competitive, Scarcity, Fear, Negative Attitude/Low Vibration, or a "-" Mindset, correct it immediately.

Everything you see on earth is made from one Universal Original Intelligent Thinking Substance, out of which all things are made.

Thoughts Make things.

Thoughts Create things.

Thoughts are on Frequencies, and they are all interconnected.

Thoughts travel faster than the speed of light.

Thoughts travel through any and all mass.

New forms are constantly being made, and older ones are dissolving, but all are shapes assumed by One Thing.

There is no limit to the supply of Universal Original Formless Intelligent Substance. The entire Universe is made out of It, but It was not all used eons and eons ago in the original creation of the Universe. The spaces in, through, and between the forms of the visible Universe are permeated and filled with the Original Substance, with the Formless Intelligence, with the Original Raw Material of all Raw Materials and of all things. Billions of times as much as has been made might still be made, and even then, we would not exhaust the supply of Universal Raw Material.

You, therefore, are never poor because nature is never poor, or because you think there is not enough to go around.

Again, you do not Live in a zero-sum world or Universe.

You live in a Universe of *unlimited abundance*.

Universal Intelligence has seen to it that nature is an inexhaustible storehouse of riches for you and that the supply will never run short. Original Substance is alive with creative, expressive, expansive, increasing, Manifesting, and growth-minded energy, and it is constantly producing more forms. When the supply of building material is exhausted, more will be produced. When the soil is exhausted so that foodstuffs and materials for clothing will no longer grow in it, it will be renewed or more soil will be made. When all the gold and silver has been dug from the earth, if we are still in such a stage of social development that we need gold and silver, more will be produced from the Formless Intelligent Substance, for the Universal Formless Intelligent Thinking Substance responds to your needs, and it will not let you be without any good thing you desire and acquire through the Universal Way and according to Universal Laws.

This is true of us collectively, for people as a whole are always abundantly rich, and if individuals are poor, it is because they do not follow the Universal Way of doing things that makes the individual person successful.

The Formless Substance is Intelligent. It is a Universal Substance that thinks. It is alive, and it is always impelled toward more expression, expansion, increase, Manifesting, growth, and life.

It is the natural and inherent impulse of life to seek to live more. It is the nature of Universal Intelligence to enlarge Itself, and of Consciousness to seek to extend Its boundaries and find fuller expression. The Universe of Forms have been made by Universal Intelligent Living Substance, throwing Itself into Form in order to Express Itself more fully.

The Universe is a great Living Presence, always moving inherently toward more life and fuller functioning.

Universal Intelligence Formed nature for the advancement of life, and *Its impelling motive is the Increase of Life*. For this cause, everything that can possibly minister to life is bountifully provided. There can be no lack unless Universal Intelligence is to contradict Itself and nullify Its own works and Its own Universal Laws.

Know that you are not kept poor by lack in the supply of opportunity or riches. It is a fact that I shall discuss a little further on that the resources of the Universal Formless Supply are at your immediate command when you will think, feel, and act in the Universal Way.

Chapter 1:

Your First Principle in the Universal Intelligence Science of Success and Happiness... "Thought"

"You are what you think. So just think big, believe big, act big, work big, give big, forgive big, laugh big, love big, and live big."
—Andrew Carnegie

"You do not live in a zero-sum world, quite the contrary, you live in a 'Thought World,' within a Perfect and Infinite 'Thought Universe,' filled with unlimited abundance. The 'Thought Universe' you live in was filled for your enjoyment by Universal Intelligence with infinite wisdom, love, life, abundance, joy, and harmony."
—P. J. DiNuzzo

THOUGHT *is the only power* that can call into existence and produce your goal and tangible riches from the Universal Intelligent Formless Thinking Substance. The Original Intelligent Substance from which all things are made *is a Substance that Thinks,* **and a "thought of form" in this Substance produces the thought-form.**

Original Substance moves according to its thoughts. Every form and process you see in nature is the visible expression of a thought in Original Substance. As the Formless Substance thinks of a form, it takes that form; as it thinks of a motion, it makes that motion.

This is the way all things in the history of the Universe were and are created. Know, and never forget or waver, that you live in a *thought world,* which is an integrated part of a perfect and infinite *thought universe.*

The concept of a moving and expanding Universe extended throughout Formless Substance, and the Thinking Substance, moving according to that thought, originally took the form of systems of planets and maintains that form.

Holding the idea of a circling system of suns and worlds, It takes the form of these bodies and moves them as It Thinks. Thinking the form of a slow-growing oak tree, It moves accordingly and produces the tree, though centuries may be required to do the work. In creating, the Formless Intelligent Substance typically moves according to the lines of motion It has previously established. The thought of an oak tree does not cause the instant formation of a full-grown tree, but it does start in motion the forces that will produce the tree, along established lines of growth.

Every thought of form (thought-form) held in Thinking Universal Original Substance causes the creation of the form, generally along the lines of growth and action already established.

The thought of a house of a certain construction, if it were impressed upon Formless Substance, might not cause the instant formation of the house, but it would cause the turning of creative energies already working in trade and commerce into such channels as to result in the speedy building of the house. And if there were no existing channels through which the creative energy could work, then the house would be formed directly from primal substance, without waiting for the slow processes of the organic and inorganic world.

No thought-form can be impressed upon Universal Original Substance without initiating and ultimately causing the creation of the form.

Your Mind is a Divine Operation and Thinking Center, and you possess the power to originate thought and create your own original thought-forms. All the forms that you fashion with your hands must first exist in your thought and in your mind; you cannot shape a thing until you first have thought that thing.

Predominately, historically, people have unfortunately confined their efforts wholly to the work of their hands as they have applied manual labor to the world of forms, seeking to change or modify those already existing. Very few have thought of trying to cause the creation of new thought-forms by Co-Creating and impressing their thoughts upon Universal Formless Substance.

When you have a thought-form, you take material from the forms of nature and make an image of the form that is in your mind. You have, so far in your life, made little or no effort to cooperate with Formless Intelligence or to work as a Co-Creator with Universal Intelligence. People are reshaping and modifying existing forms through manual labor, while giving no attention to the question of whether they may produce things from Formless Substance by communicating their thoughts to It. I will teach you that you may do so, and I will teach any of my fellow brothers or sisters to do so as well.

As my first step, I will lay down the following propositions.

First, I assert that there is one Universal Original Thinking Formless Substance, from which all things are made. All the seemingly many elements are but different presentations of this One Element. All the many forms found in organic and inorganic nature are but different shapes, made from the same Original Substance.

And this Substance is a Thinking Substance—a thought held in It produces the thought-form of the thought.

Thought, in Thinking Substance, produces shapes. Your mind is a thinking center empowered by Divine Operation, capable of Creative Original Thought. If you can communicate your thought to Original Thinking Substance, you can cause the creation, or formation, of the thing you think about.

To summarize:

There is a Universal Intelligent Original Thinking Substance from which all things are made, and which, in Its original state, permeates, penetrates, and fills the interspaces of the entire Universe.

Your thought in this Substance produces the thought-form and thing that you visualize in your thought.

You can form things in your thought, and by impressing your thought-form upon Universal Intelligent Thinking Substance, you can cause the thing you think about to be created.

Know it, and know it in your heart of hearts that this is the foundation of the Universal Way and your path to Manifesting the goal of your dreams and wishes.

I have said that our fellow brothers and sisters succeed, Manifest, and live their Best-Life by doing things in the Universal Way, and in order to do so, they must become able to think in the Universal Way.

I promise you; this is an all-powerful life changer for you.

It is exactly, as you know deep inside of you, what you have been waiting for.

Your way of doing things is the direct result of the way you think about things.

To do things in the way you want to do them, you will have to acquire the ability to think the way you want to think. This is the first step toward success and Manifesting your goal.

To think what you want to think is to think TRUTH, *inside-out*, regardless of appearances, *outside-in*.

I will teach you and show you Universal Intelligence's TRUTH and coach you until you embrace it with your thought, mind, imagination, burning-desire, emotion, and action.

You have the natural and inherent power to think what you want to think. *You* possess the power of true *free will,* but it requires far more effort to do so than it does to think the thoughts that are suggested by outward appearances, *outside-in,* and that come to you through other people and things, your ego, and your five senses (sight, smell, taste, hearing, and touch).

To think *outside-in* according to appearances is easy, but to think TRUTH *inside-out* through your mind, regardless of outward appearances, is laborious, and it requires the expenditure of more Higher-Faculty WIP RIM (Will, Imagination, Perception, Reason, Intuition, Memory) power than any other work you are called upon to perform.

There is no labor from which most people shrink as much as they do from that of sustained and consecutive thought, for it can be the hardest work in the world to a lot of people. This is especially true when TRUTH, *inside-out,* is contrary to *outside* appearances.

Every appearance in the visible world, *outside-in,* tends to produce a corresponding form in your mind as you observe it, and this can only be prevented by you holding the thought of the Universal TRUTH in your mind.

To look upon the appearance of disease will produce the form of disease in your own mind, and ultimately in your body, unless you hold the thought of the TRUTH, which is that there is no disease; it is only an appearance, and Universal reality is health.

Never forget, your Spiritual Spark is Perfect, your Spiritual DNA is Perfect, and your Spirit is Perfect.

For they are the real you.

You are an Eternal Spiritual Being having a limited physical experience.

You are an *energy source* and an *energy field* living within a larger energy source and energy field. You are connected to the entire Universe and Its One Energy Field.

You are an infinite energy field with Co-Creator powers resulting in infinite and unfolding possibilities for yourself.

You truly have no restrictions or limitations.

You are source energy, and this enables you to Co-Create with the Universe and Universal Intelligence.

To look upon the appearances of poverty will produce corresponding forms in your own mind unless you hold to the TRUTH that there is no poverty; there is only abundance.

To think health when surrounded by the appearances of disease, or to think riches when in the midst or appearances of poverty, requires focus and power, but as you acquire this power, you become a *mastermind*. You can conquer fate and you can *Manifest Anything You Can Imagine*.

This power can only be acquired by getting hold of the basic fact that is behind all appearances, and that fact is that there is one Original Universal Thinking Substance, from which and by which all things are made.

Then you must grasp the TRUTH that every thought you hold in this Original Substance becomes a thought-form, and that you can so impress your thoughts upon It so as to cause them to take form and become visible things.

Every single thought of yours begins to and generates a thought-form.

Thinking Substance takes the form of Its Thought and moves according to the thought.

Thoughts Create things.

Thoughts Make things.

Thoughts Become things.

You attract and become what you Think about most often.

The Law of Attraction Manifests the thing that you think about (both good and bad).

Thoughts are like *individual pictures*—they are powerful and Manifest your goal.

Thoughts and your pictures connected together and visualized like a *short film* will Manifest your goal faster.

Thoughts and your pictures connected together and visualized with emotion like a *full-length movie* will Manifest your goal fastest.

Thoughts create energy, energy creates matter, matter creates things.

You and I get to protect our Subconscious Minds, which I refer to as your "Magic Lamp," (and "P. J.'s Magic Lamp" when I talk about my Subconscious Mind). And we aspire to *reject* or *cancel* any and all "negative suggestions" from ourselves, others, or outside sources, into our Subconscious Minds at all costs.

Always do everything you possibly can to maintain your "Buoyancy" and your Highest- Vibration possible.

When you realize this, you lose all doubt and fear, for when you know the TRUTH and learn to live *inside-out,* and you know that you are a Co-Creator with Universal Intelligence and can create what you want to create, you can get what you want to have and can become all that you want to be. As a first step toward succeeding and Manifesting your goal, you must believe the fundamental statements I gave previously in this chapter, and in order to emphasize them, I will repeat them here:

There is a Universal Original Intelligent Thinking Substance from which all things are made, and which, in Its original state, permeates, penetrates, and fills the interspaces of the entire Universe.

Your thought in this Substance produces the thought-form and thing that you image by your thought.

You can form things in your thought, and by impressing your thought-form upon Universal Intelligent Formless Substance, you can cause the thing you think about to be created.

Know it, and know it in your heart of hearts that this is the foundation of the Universal Way and your path to Manifesting the goal of your dreams and wishes.

I implore you to *focus* and lay aside all other concepts of the Universe other than this Supreme One. You must dwell upon this until it is fixed and burned into your mind and has become your ritual and habitual thought. Read my creed statements over and over again, fix every word in your memory, and meditate upon them until you firmly and absolutely believe what they say. If a doubt comes to you, cast it aside as a falsehood. Do not listen to arguments against this idea. Do not go to presentations or lectures where a contrary concept of things is taught or promoted. Do not read books, engage on social media, or listen to others that teach a different Idea. If you get mixed up in your Faith, all your efforts will be in vain.

Do not ask why these things are true, nor speculate as to how they can be true; simply take them on trust with me.

Right now, it is not necessary that you believe in everything I am teaching you and in yourself 100 percent.

All that is necessary right now for your success is that you know that I believe in you 100 percent.

The Universal Laws and Science to *Manifest Anything You Can Imagine* begin with the absolute acceptance of this Faith.

Chapter 5:

Universal Intelligence's "Perpetual Increase of Life"

"All you can possibly need or desire is already yours. You need no helper to give it to you; it is yours now. Call your desires into being by imagining and feeling your wish fulfilled. As the end is accepted, you become totally indifferent as to possible failure, for acceptance of the end wills the means to that end."
—Neville Goddard

"Believe and know in your heart of hearts that Universal Intelligence longs for you to have everything you want and desire in life and to Manifest and live your Best-Life. Universal Intelligence has set your table in front of you for you to express, expand, increase, grow, succeed, Manifest, and fulfill your dreams and wishes by living your Best-Life. Step into your new 1 percent better self every single morning and co-create with It. This is Universal Intelligence's primal desire for you."
—P. J. DiNuzzo

Y ou must get rid of the last vestige of the old idea that there is a Universal Power whose will it is that you should be poor, or whose purposes may be served by keeping you in poverty.

The Intelligent Substance that is All, and in All, and that lives in All *and lives in you,* is a consciously Living Substance. Being a consciously Living Substance, It must have the natural and inherent desire of every Living Intelligence for increase of life. Every living thing must continually seek for the enlargement of its life because life, in the mere act of living, must increase itself.

A seed dropped into the ground springs into activity, and in the act of living, it produces a hundred more seeds. Life, by living, multiplies itself. It is forever becoming more. It must do so if it continues to be at all.

Universal Intelligence is under this same necessity for continuous increase. Every thought you think makes it necessary for you to think another thought. Consciousness is continually expanding. Every fact you learn leads you to the learning of another fact. Knowledge is continually increasing. Every talent you cultivate brings to your mind the desire to cultivate another talent. You are subject to the urge of life, seeking expression, which drives you on to know more, do more, and be more.

In order to know more, do more, and be more, you must and can have more. You must have things to use, for you learn and do and become, only by enjoying things. You must succeed, Manifest, be happy, and enjoy life and continue to further express, expand, increase, and grow so that you can be in a Higher-Vibration enjoying and living in harmony with Universal Intelligence.

The desire to succeed and be happy is simply the capacity for larger life seeking fulfillment.

Every desire is the effort of an unexpressed possibility striving to come into action.

It is power seeking to Manifest, which causes desire. That which makes you want more success and happiness is the same as that which makes the plant grow. It is life seeking fuller expression.

The One Living Substance must be and is subject to this Universal and Inherent Law of all life. It is permeated with the desire to live more. That is why it is under Universal Intelligence's necessity of creating things.

The One Substance Desires to live, express, expand, increase, and grow more in you, so It truly wants you to have all the things you can use and properly enjoy.

It is the desire of Universal Intelligence that you should be happy and enjoy success. Universal Intelligence wants this for you because It can express Itself better through you if you have plenty of things to use in giving It expression. Universal Intelligence can live more in you if you Co-Create with It and have unlimited command of the means of life.

Believe and know in your heart of hearts that Universal Intelligence longs for you to have everything you want and desire In life and to Manifest and live your Best-Life.

Nature is abundantly friendly to your wants, desires, wishes, and dreams.

Everything is naturally for you.

Make up your mind that this is true.

It is essential, however, that your purpose should harmonize with the purpose that is in all of us.

You must want real life, not mere pleasure or sensual gratification. Life is the performance of function, and you really live only when you perform every function—physical, mental, emotional, heartfelt, and Spiritual—of which you are capable, without excess in any.

You do not want to succeed in order to live swinishly, for the gratification of animal desires is not life. But the performance of every physical function is a part of life, and no one lives completely who denies the impulses of the body a normal and healthful expression.

You do not want to succeed solely to enjoy mental pleasures, get knowledge, gratify ambition, outshine others, or be famous. All these are a part of life, but the person who lives for the pleasures of the intellect alone will only have a partial life, and they will never be satisfied with their lot.

You do not want to succeed solely for the good of others, to lose yourself for the salvation of humankind, or to experience the joys of charity and sacrifice. The joys of the Spirit are only a part of life, and they are no better or more noble than any other part.

You want to succeed in order that you may eat, drink, and be merry when it is time to do these things, in order that you may surround yourself with beautiful things, see distant lands, feed your mind, and develop your intellect, and in order that you may Love others and do kind things, expand your Spirit, and be able to play a good part in helping your fellow brothers and sisters find TRUTH, wisdom, love, life, abundance, joy, and harmony.

But remember that extreme altruism is no better and no nobler than extreme selfishness. Both are mistakes.

Get rid of the idea that Universal Intelligence wants you to sacrifice yourself for others, and that you can secure Its favor by doing so.

That is a scarcity mindset.

Universal Intelligence desires and requires nothing of the kind.

What Universal Intelligence wants is that you should make the most of yourself, for yourself and for others, and *you can help others more by making the most of yourself than in any other way.*

You can make the most of yourself only by succeeding at enjoying your Best-Life and growing, so it is right and praiseworthy that you should give your first and best thought to the work of acquiring wealth, health, and happiness.

Remember, however, that the desire of Universal Intelligent Substance is for all, and Its movements must be for *more life to all.* It cannot be made to work for less life to any because It is equally in all, seeking success, riches, expansion, increase, and life.

Intelligent Substance will make things for you, but it will *not* take things away from someone else and give them to you.

To *truly* succeed, you must always remain in a Creative Mindset, never a Competitive one.

You must get rid of the thought of Competition along with envy, hatred, and jealousy.

You are to Create, not to Compete, for what the Universe has available for you and you are to do so in a *mindset of abundance*.

You do not have to take anything away from anyone to have what you desire.

You do not have to drive sharp bargains. You do not have to cheat, lie, or take advantage of others. You do not need to let any man or woman work for you for less than they earn.

You do not have to covet the property of others, or look at it with wishful eyes. No man or woman has anything of which you cannot have the like, so you do not need to consider or take action to take what they have away from them.

You are to become a *Creator, a Co-Creator, with Universal Intelligence, NOT a Competitor*. You are going to get what you want, but in such a way that when you receive it, every other person you interact with who assists you will have more than they have now.

The Universe is aligned with Creation and *never* aligned with Competition.

I am aware that there are some people who get a vast amount of money by proceeding in direct opposition to my statements above, and I may add a word of explanation here. Men and women of a certain type who become successful or very rich, do so sometimes purely through their extraordinary ability on the plane of Competition, and sometimes they unconsciously relate themselves to

Universal Substance in its great purposes and movements for the general population.

Riches and success secured on the Competitive plane, however, are *never satisfactory and permanent.* They are yours today, and another's tomorrow. Remember, if you are to succeed according to Universal Laws in a Scientific Universal Way, you must rise *entirely* out of Competitive Thought onto the higher plane of a Creative Mindset.

You must *never* think in a Scarcity Mindset for a moment that the supply is limited.

To succeed at Manifesting your dreams and wishes, you are always to remain in a *mindset of abundance.*

Just as soon as you begin to think that all the money is being "cornered" and controlled by bankers and others, and that you must exert yourself to get laws passed to stop this process, and so on, in that moment, you drop into the Competitive Mind, and your power to cause creation is gone for the time being. What is worse, you will probably arrest the wonderful creative movements you have already launched.

Know that there are countless billions of dollars worth of gold in the mountains on earth, not yet brought to light, and know that if there were not, more would be created from Original Thinking Substance to supply your and other's needs.

Know that the money you need will come, even if it is necessary for a thousand people to be led to the discovery of new gold mines tomorrow.

Never look at the visible supply. Look always at the limitless riches in Universal Original Formless Substance. Always look at the TRUTH and *know* that when you Manifest in the Universal Way, your goal is coming to you as fast as you can receive it and use it.

Nobody, by cornering the visible supply, can prevent you from getting what is yours.

So *never* allow yourself to think for an instant that all the best building spots will be taken before you get ready to build your house unless you hurry. Never worry about the controlling entities and get anxious for fear they will soon come to own the whole earth. Never be afraid that you will lose what you want because some other person "beats you to it." That cannot possibly happen. You are not seeking anything that is possessed by anybody else; you are causing what you want to be created from Original Formless Thinking Substance, and Its supply is without limits.

Commit yourself to my formulated statement:

There is a Universal Original Intelligent Thinking Substance from which all things are made, and which, in Its original state, permeates, penetrates, and fills the interspaces of the entire Universe.

Your thought in this Substance produces the thought-form and thing that you image by your thought.

You can form things in your thought, and by impressing your thought-form upon Universal Intelligence Original Thinking Substance, you can cause the thing you think about to be created.

Chapter 6:

How Your Manifested Goal and Success Come to You through Universal Intelligence

"Assume the feeling of your wish fulfilled and continue feeling that it is fulfilled until that which you feel objectifies itself...."
—Neville Goddard

"It happened around five years ago, but it's sort of like a mantra. You repeat it to yourself every day. 'Music is my life. Music is my life. The fame is inside of me. I'm going to make a number one record with number one hits.' And it's not yet, it's a lie. You're saying a lie over and over and over again, but then one day, the lie is true."
—Lady Gaga

"Thoughts are like pictures, they are powerful and Manifest your goal. Thoughts and your pictures connected together and visualized like a short film will Manifest your goal faster. Thoughts and your pictures connected together and visualized with emotion like a movie will Manifest your goal fastest."
—P. J. DiNuzzo

When I say that you do not have to drive sharp bargains, I do not mean that you do not have to drive any bargains at all, or that you are above the necessity for having any dealings with your fellow brothers and sisters. I mean that you will not need to deal with them unfairly. You do not have to get something for nothing, *but you can and should give to every person more than you take from them.*

You should *always* strive to provide your fellow brothers and sisters with the "Impression of Increase" and deliver a Use Value that is higher than the Cash Value you receive from them.

You cannot give every person more in Cash Value than you take from them, but you can give them more in Use Value than the Cash Value of the thing you receive from them. The paper, ink, and other material in my book may not be worth the money you paid for it, but if the ideas suggested by it bring you thousands or millions of dollars, you have not been wronged by those who sold it to you. They have given you a great Use Value for a small Cash Value.

When you rise from the Competitive to the Creative plane, you can scan your business transactions very easily, and if you are selling any person anything that does not add more to their life than the thing they give you in exchange, you can and should immediately afford to stop it. You do not have to beat anybody in business. And if you are in a business that does beat people, *get out of it today.*

If you give every man and woman more in Use Value than you take from them in Cash Value, then you are in harmony with Universal Intelligence, adding to the life of the world with every business transaction you touch.

Universal Intelligence will love you for this.

If you have people working for you, you must take from them more in Cash Value than you pay them in wages, but you can organize your business so that it is an excellent business filled with the principle of advancement, so that each employee and team member who wishes to do so may advance a little every day.

You can make your business do for your employees and team members what my book is doing for you. You can conduct your business so that it will be a sort of ladder, by which every team member who will take the effort may climb to their desired success themself, given the opportunity, and if they make a personal choice not to do so, it is not your fault.

And finally, because you are to cause the creation of your success from Universal Intelligent Thinking Substance that permeates all your environment, it does not follow that they are to take shape from the atmosphere and come into being before your eyes.

If you want a smartphone or computer, for instance, I do not mean to tell you that you are to impress the thought of the smartphone or computer on Thinking Substance until they are formed without hands, in the room where you sit, or elsewhere. But if you want the smartphone or computer, hold the mental image of it with the most positive certainty that it is being made, or is on its way to you, or ideally that you currently physically possess and enjoy it. After once forming the thought, have the most absolute and unquestioning Faith that the smartphone or computer is coming. Never think of it, or speak of it, in any other way than as being sure it will arrive.

Claim it and constantly think of it and enjoy it as already yours.

Always carry with you through your speech, visualization, and emotion the "assumption of your wish fulfilled."

"I AM so Happy and Grateful now that I bask in the Gratitude of the Assumption of my Wish Fulfilled."

It will be brought to you by the power of Universal Intelligence, acting upon the minds of men and women. If you live in Maine, it may be that a man or woman will be brought into contact with you from Texas or Australia to engage in some transaction that will result in your getting what you want and desire.

If so, the whole matter will be as much to that person's advantage as it is to yours.

Do not forget for a moment that Universal Intelligent Thinking Substance is through all, in all, communicating with all, and can influence all. The desire of Thinking Substance for fuller expression, expansion, increase, growth, life, and happiness has caused the creation of all the smartphones and computers already made, and it can cause the creation of millions or billions more, and it will, whenever men and women set it in motion by a burning-desire and Faith and by acting in the Universal Way in harmony with Universal Laws.

You can certainly have a smartphone or computer in your house, and it is just as certain that you can have any other thing or things you want that you will use for the advancement of your own life and the lives of others.

You *never* need to hesitate to ask.

Universal Intelligence is virtually begging for you to ask and has your table completely set for you to enjoy.

Original Substance wants to Co-Create with you and live all that is possible in you, and it wants you to have all that you can or will use for the living of your most abundant life.

If you fix upon your Consciousness the fact that the desire you feel for success is one with the desire of Universal Intelligence for more complete expression, your Faith becomes invincible.

Once there was a little boy sitting at a piano, vainly trying to bring harmony out of the keys, who was upset by his inability to play real music. When asked the cause of his frustration, he answered, "I can feel the music in me, but I can't make my hands go right." The music in him was the *urge* of Universal Intelligence Original Thinking Substance, containing all the possibilities of all life. All that there is of music was seeking expression through the child at that moment.

Universal Intelligence, right now, at this very moment, is trying to live and do and enjoy things through you and all humanity. Universal Intelligence is saying, "I want hands to build wonderful structures, to play divine harmonies, to paint glorious pictures. I want feet to run my errands, eyes to see my beauties, tongues to tell mighty truths and to sing marvelous songs."

All that there is of possibility is seeking expression through *all* men and women. Universal Intelligence wants those who can play music to have pianos and every other instrument, and to have the means to cultivate their talents to their fullest extent. It wants those who can appreciate beauty to be able to surround themselves with beautiful things. It wants those who can discern truth to have every opportunity to travel and observe. It wants those who can appreciate dress to be beautifully clothed, and those who can appreciate good food to be luxuriously fed.

Universal Intelligence wants all these things because It, Itself, enjoys and appreciates them. It is Universal Intelligence that wants to Co-Create with you to play, and sing, and enjoy beauty, and proclaim truth, and wear fine clothes, and eat good food.

The desire you feel for success, health, wealth, happiness, and your Best-Life is the Infinite inside of you, seeking to express Itself in you as It sought to find expression in that little boy at the piano.

So you never need to hesitate to ask largely.

Your part is to focus on and express your desires to Universal Intelligence. This is a difficult point for most people, for they retain something of the old idea that poverty and self-sacrifice are pleasing. They look upon poverty as a part of some plan, a necessity of nature. They have the false idea that the majority of men and women must stay poor because there is not enough to go around. They hold on to so much of this flawed thought that they feel ashamed to ask for success and their Best-Life. They try not to want more than a very modest competence, just enough to make them fairly comfortable.

There once was a student who desired to Manifest and was told that they must get in mind a clear picture of the things they wanted so that the creative thought of them might be impressed on Universal Intelligent Formless Substance. They were very poor, living in a rented house, and having only what they earned from day to day, and they could not grasp the fact that all possible wealth was theirs. So, after thinking the matter over, they decided that they might reasonably ask for a new rug for the floor of their best room and a new furnace to heat the house during the cold winter weather. Following the instructions given by their mentor, they obtained these things in a few months, and then it dawned on them that they had not asked for enough. They went through the house in which they lived and planned all the improvements they would like to make in it, mentally adding a bay window here and a room there until it was complete in their mind as their ideal home. And then they planned its furnishings.

Holding the whole picture in their mind, they began living in the Universal Way and moving toward what they wanted. And they went on to own the house and rebuild it in the form of their mental image. And then, with still larger Faith, they went on to get even greater things. It was delivered to them according to what I refer to as P. J.'s Fifteen (15) Key Ingredient Manifest Recipe: BELIEF, FAITH, PURPOSE, THOUGHT, IMAGINATION, WANT, VISION, GOAL, BURNING-DESIRE, VISUALIZATION, EMOTION, ACTION, ACCEPTANCE, BUOY-ANCY, and GRATITUDE.

It is so with you and with all of us.

Chapter 7:
Gratitude... Gratitude... Gratitude

"If you want to be happy, set a goal that commands your thoughts, liberates your energy, and inspires your hopes."
—Andrew Carnegie

"The Law of Gratitude is a Universal Law and includes, in part, that action and reaction are always equal and in opposite directions. In other words, the Gratitude you give to Universal Intelligence is returned equally to you. Be continuously Grateful that not only does Universal Intelligence know your name, but it also truly loves you and emotionally desires for you to co-create with It and live your Best-Life, every single day."
—P. J. DiNuzzo

The illustrations I offered in my last chapter are to convey to you the fact that the first step toward living your Best-Life is to *convey the thought and idea* of your wants to Universal Intelligent Formless Substance.

This is true, and you will see that in order to do so, it becomes necessary to relate yourself to the Formless Intelligence in a harmonious way.

To secure this harmonious relationship is a matter of such primary and vital importance that I shall give some space to its discussion here, and give you instructions that, if you will follow them, will be certain to bring you into unity with Universal Intelligence.

The cornerstone of my entire process of mental adjustment and alignment with Universal Intelligence can be summed up in one word, *Gratitude*.

For every mental and physical action you take, there is an equal and opposite reaction and movement toward you.

First, you Believe that there is one Intelligent Substance, from which all things proceed. Second, you Believe that this Original Substance gives you everything you desire, and third, you relate yourself to It by a feeling of deep, emotion-filled, continuous, and profound Gratitude.

Gratitude filled with emotion is your daily key to Manifesting your dreams and wishes.

A burning-desire filled with emotion is the fuel and energy that Manifests your goal.

When visualizing your goal, your emotion should be a high vibration at the same level as that of a child's on Christmas morning.

Many people who order their lives rightly in all other ways are kept in poverty by their lack of Gratitude. Having received one gift from Universal Intelligence, they cut the wires that connect them with It by failing to make acknowledgment and show appreciation... to express genuine Gratitude.

It is easy to understand that the nearer we live to the source of wealth, the more wealth we shall receive. And it is easy also to understand that the Spirit that is always Grateful lives in closer touch and harmony with Universal Intelligence than the one that never looks to It in thankful acknowledgment.

The more Gratefully you fix your mind on Universal Intelligence when good things come to you, the more good things you will receive, and the more rapidly they will come.

The reason simply is that the mental attitude of Gratitude draws your mind into closer touch with the Universal Source from which all gifts are delivered unto you.

If it is a "New Thought" to you that Gratitude brings your whole mind into closer harmony with the creative energies of Universal Intelligence, consider it well, and you will see that it is true. The good things you already have were delivered to you by an alignment with Universal Laws. Gratitude will lead your mind out along the ways through which things come, and it will keep you in close harmony with Creative Thought and prevent you from falling into Competitive Thought.

Gratitude alone can keep you looking toward the All and prevent you from falling into the error of a Competitive, Scarcity, Fear, or Negative Attitude/Low Vibration Mindset and Thinking of the supply as limited. To do that would be fatal to your hopes.

There is a Law of Gratitude, and it is absolutely necessary that you should observe this Universal Law if you are to get the results you seek.

The Law of Gratitude is a Universal Law and includes, in part, that action and reaction are always equal and in opposite directions. In other words, the Gratitude you give to the world is returned equally to you.

The Grateful outreaching of your mind in thankful praise to Universal Intelligence is a liberation or expenditure of force. It cannot fail to reach that to which it is directed, and the reaction is an instantaneous movement toward you.

And if your Gratitude is strong and constant, the reaction in Universal Thinking Formless Substance will be strong and continuous and the movement of the things you want will be always toward you. *You cannot exercise much power without Gratitude, for it is Gratitude that keeps you connected with power.*

But the value of Gratitude does not consist solely of getting you more blessings in the future. Without Gratitude, you cannot long keep from dissatisfied thought regarding things as they are.

The moment you permit your mind to dwell with dissatisfaction upon things as they are, you begin to lose ground. You fix attention upon the common, the ordinary, the poor, and your mind takes the form of these things. Then you will transmit these forms or mental images to the Formless Substance, and the common, the poor, and the ordinary will be attracted to you and come to you.

In this state you are living your life *outside-in*, which is the exact opposite of your daily goal of living *inside-out*, in Universal Intelligence's TRUTH. Do not live your life *outside-in* by allowing people and things, your five senses, and your ego to drive your thoughts, emotions, mindset, decisions, buoyancy, and actions. Rather, live your life by the TRUTH, *inside-out*, in control, knowing that you are in control of your life as a Co-Creator with Universal Intelligence.

To permit your mind to dwell upon Scarcity and the inferior is to become inferior and to surround yourself with inferior things.

On the other hand, to fix your attention on abundance and the best is to surround yourself with abundance and the best, and to become the best.

As Bob Proctor stated, "See yourself living in abundance and you will attract it. It always works. It works every time with every person."

The creative power within us makes us into the Image of that to which we give our attention.

You possess within yourself a Perfect Spiritual Spark, Perfect Spirit, and Perfect Spiritual DNA of Universal Thinking Substance that are truly the real you, and this all-powerful Thinking Substance *always* takes the form of that about which It thinks.

Never forget, you are an eternal Spiritual Being with Perfect Spiritual DNA currently having a limited Physical experience Living in your "meat suit."

The Grateful mind is constantly fixed upon the best; therefore, it tends to become the best. It takes the form or character of the best, and it will receive the best.

Like Attracts Like.

Also, Faith is born of Gratitude. The Grateful mind continually expects good things, and expectation becomes Faith. The reaction of Gratitude upon one's own mind produces Faith, and every outgoing wave of Grateful appreciation increases Faith. The person who has no feeling of Gratitude cannot long retain a living Faith, and without a living Faith, you cannot succeed and get to live your Best-Life by the Universal Creative Method, as you will see in my following chapters.

It is necessary, then, to cultivate the habit of being Grateful for every good thing that comes to you, and to give thanks continuously.

And because all things have contributed to your advancement, you should include all things in your Gratitude.

If you give emotion-filled Gratitude for the roof over your head, the food on your table, and the clothes on your back, you will continue to abundantly receive those blessings.

Do not waste time thinking or talking about the shortcomings or wrong actions of controlling entities. Their organization of the world has made your opportunity. All you get really comes to you because of them.

Do not rage against corrupt politicians. If it were not for politicians, we would fall into anarchy, and your opportunity would be greatly lessened.

Always strive to remain neutral.

Even when you are at your "worst," give your full effort to never let your vibration fall below neutral.

Universal Intelligence has worked for a very long time, and with extreme patience, to bring us up to where we are in economics, industry, commerce, and government. And It is going right on with Its work. There is not the least doubt that It will do away with monopolists, captains of industry, controlling entities, and corrupt politicians as soon as they can be spared. But, in the meantime, behold that they are all very good. Remember that they are all helping to arrange the lines of transmission along which your success, health, wealth, Manifesting, happiness, and living your Best-Life come to you, and be Grateful to them all. This will bring you into harmonious relations with the good in everything, and the good in everything will move toward you.

Always forgive, and do so with love, anyone who has ever harmed you or even intended to harm you. And then release these individuals—and yourself—from your thoughts.

Chapter 8:
Thinking in the Universal Way

"The intuitive [Subconscious] mind is a sacred gift and the rational [Conscious] mind is a faithful servant. We have created a society that honors the servant and has forgotten the gift."
—Albert Einstein

"There is a power under your control that is greater than poverty, greater than the lack of education, greater than all your fears and superstitions combined. It is the power to take possession of your own mind and to direct it to whatever ends you may desire."
—Andrew Carnegie

"There is an abundance of opportunity for you to go with the tide, instead of trying to swim against it. Always find the direction of the flow and ride it. Let It and Universal Intelligence do the work for you and Co-Create with them."
—P. J. DiNuzzo

Turn back to chapter 6, and read again the story of the person who formed a mental image of their house, and you will get a fair Idea of the initial step toward success, health, wealth, happiness, and Manifesting your Best-Life.

You must form a clear and definite mental picture of what you want. You cannot transmit an idea unless you have it yourself, clearly on the screen of your mind. Remember, you live in a *thought world* within a perfect and infinite *thought Universe.*

To succeed, you must first think a *thought* and create a *thought-form* and idea in your Conscious Mind as a *want,* and then with proper commitment, *emotionally* push it, *with the same level of emotion as a child on Christmas morning,* and deposit it into the "Treasury" of your Subconscious mind as a *desire.*

Resultingly, if you desire it *intensely* enough, so much so that it is a burning-desire, your body, which is an "instrument of your mind," will emit the proper vibrations *and* begin to take action toward meeting your goal.

To Manifest, you first create your goal in your mind and then you access the "physical-back" of it with your actions.

You must have it before you can give it, and many people fail to impress Thinking Substance because they have only a vague and misty concept of the things they want to do, have, or become.

You truly need to focus, have discipline, *stay true to your ritual,* and perform the repetitions in order to <u>*Manifest Anything* You Can Imagine</u>.

It is not enough that you should have a general desire for wealth "to do good with." Everybody has that desire.

It is not enough that you should have a wish to travel, see things, live more, etc. Everybody has those desires also. If you were going to text a message to a friend, you would not send the letters of the alphabet in their order and let them construct the message for themselves. Nor would you take words at random from the dictionary. You would send a coherent sentence, one that meant something. When you try to impress your wants upon Universal Intelligent Thinking Substance, remember that it must be done through a coherent statement and image. You must know what you want, be definite, focused, and disciplined, and apply consistent repetitions.

You can never enjoy success and start the creative power into action by sending out unformed longings and vague desires.

Go over your desires just as the person I have described went over their house, see just what you want, and get a clear mental picture of it on the screen of your mind as you wish it to look when you receive it.

That clear mental picture you must have continually in your mind, as the sailor has in their mind the port toward which they are sailing their ship. You must keep your face toward it all the time. You must no more lose sight of it than the captain loses sight of their compass.

All you need is to know what you want, and to want it intensely enough that it will stay in your thoughts and Subconscious Mind as a burning-desire filled with emotion.

Spend as much of your leisure time as you can in contemplating and visualizing your picture. But no one needs to take exercises to concentrate their mind on a thing they really want and possess a burning-desire for.

A "vision board" serves as a great complement to your daily "spaced-repetition" ritual.

And unless you really want to enjoy success, so that the desire is strong enough to hold your Thoughts directed to the purpose as the magnetic pole holds the needle of the compass, it will hardly be worthwhile for you to try to carry out the instructions given in my book.

The methods I set forth are for people whose desire for success, health, wealth, relationships, happiness, and yearning to Manifest their dreams and wishes is strong enough to overcome mental laziness and the love of ease and make them work.

The clearer and more definite you make your thought-form picture, and the more you dwell upon it, bringing out all its delightful details, the stronger your desire will be. And the stronger your burning-desire, the easier it will be to hold your mind fixed upon the picture of what you want and live in its TRUTH, as if you are already in physical possession of it.

Something more is necessary, however, than merely seeing the picture clearly. If that is all you do, you are only a dreamer, and you will have little or no power for accomplishment.

Behind your clear vision containing your goal must be your purpose to realize it, to bring it out in tangible expression.

And behind this purpose must be an invincible and unwavering FAITH THAT THE THING IS ALREADY YOURS, that it is "in your hand," and that you have already taken possession of it.

Always live with deep emotion in your TRUTH from an "assumption of your wish fulfilled."

Live in the new house, mentally, until it takes form around you physically. In the mental realm, enter at once into full enjoyment of the things you want.

See the things you want as if they are actually around you all the time. See yourself as owning, using, and enjoying them. Make use of them in your imagination just as you will use them when they are your tangible possessions. Dwell upon your mental picture until it is clear and distinct. Then take the mental attitude of ownership toward everything in that picture. Take possession of it in your mind, in the full Faith that it is actually yours.

Hold on to this mental ownership and *never* waver for an instant in the Faith that it is real.

And remember what I said in a preceding chapter about your Gratitude. Be as thankful for it *all the time* as you expect to be when it has taken physical form and is in your possession.

The person who can sincerely thank Universal Intelligence for the things that as yet they own only in imagination has real Belief and Faith;

thus, they will succeed and enjoy their Best-Life because they will cause the creation of whatever they want and desire.

Your part is to intelligently formulate your desire for the things that make up your larger life, get these desires arranged into a coherent whole, and then impress this whole burning-desire upon the Universal Intelligent Thinking Substance, which has the power and the will to bring you what you want.

You do not make this impression by repeating strings of words; you make it by holding your vision with unshakable PURPOSE to attain it, and with steadfast FAITH that you will attain it.

The answer to your desire is not according to your Faith while you are talking, but according to your Faith while you are living.

You cannot impress upon the mind of Universal Intelligence by being inconsistent.

Focus, repetition, and discipline are the keys.

Hold steadily to your vision, with the purpose of causing its creation into solid form and the Faith that you are doing so.

Always Believe that you have already received and are enjoying your desire, goal, dream, wish, and Best-Life.

The whole matter turns on acceptance and receiving once you have clearly formed your vision. When you *have* formed it, it is well to make an oral statement, properly addressing Universal Intelligence, and from that moment you must, in your mind, receive what you ask for. Live in the new house. Wear the fine clothes. Ride in the automobile. Go on the journey. Bask in your health. Enjoy the companionship. And confidently plan for greater vacations.

Think, act, and speak of all the things you have asked for in terms of actual *present* ownership.

Imagine an environment and a financial condition exactly as you want them, and live all of your time in that imaginary environment and financial condition.

Remember, however, that you do not do this as a mere dreamer and castle builder. Hold to the BELIEF and FAITH that the imaginary is tangible and real and being realized, and to your PURPOSE of realizing it. Remember that it is Faith and Purpose in the use of the imagination that make the difference between the scientist and the dreamer. And having learned this fact, it is here that you must learn the proper use of will, focus, discipline, and repetition.

Chapter 9:

How to Use Your Will to Manifest Your Goal

"Any idea that is held in the mind, that is emphasized, that is either feared or revered, will begin at once to clothe itself in the most convenient and appropriate physical forms available."
—Andrew Carnegie

"When I was very young I visualized myself being and having what it was I wanted. Mentally I never had any doubts about it. The mind is really so incredible. Before I won my first Mr. Universe title, I walked around the tournament like I owned it. The title was already mine. I had won it so many times in my mind that there was no doubt I would win it. Then when I moved on to the movies, the same thing. I visualized myself being a famous actor and earning big money. I could feel and taste success. I just knew it would all happen."
—Arnold Schwarzenegger

"When visualizing your goal your emotion should be
a high vibration at the same level as that of a child's on
Christmas morning. To Manifest, you must join with your
Inner Child and forget what you have been taught and
become one with your Inner Child of imagination."
—P. J. DiNuzzo

Your "Will" is one of six "Higher (Mental) Faculties" WIP RIM (Will, Imagination, Perception, Reason, Intuition, Memory) that is the most important element that empowers you to succeed at maintaining your focus.

A highly developed will along with focus, discipline, and repetition allows you to shut down the *outside-in* challenges from your five senses (sight, smell, taste, hearing, and touch), your ego, people, things, social media, TV, news, and focus on your goal. Purpose, burning-desire, a plan with continuous action, a positive mind and positive attitude, and accountability, all rely on persistence and your will to succeed.

A habit is an idea planted into your subjective Subconscious Mind that has been suggested so often that it automatically takes over and directs your action.

Your habits will make you or break you.

It is always only "you vs. you."

You are your only problem, and you are your only solution.

Develop the habit of persistence to maintain your will, focus, discipline, and repetition. Persisting and maintaining your will through thick and thin is one of the most important habits you must develop to succeed at Manifesting your dreams and wishes.

Goals are not to "get." Rather, they are to "grow."

To set about success, health, wealth, happiness, and Manifesting your Best-Life in a Universal Scientific Way through the Universal Way, you never try to apply your willpower to anything outside of yourself.

You have no right to do so.

It is wrong and foolhardy to attempt to apply your will to other men and women, in order to get them to do what you wish done.

You have no right to use your willpower upon another person, even "for their own good," for you do not know what is for their good.

The Universal Science of success and enjoying your Best-Life does not require you to apply power or force to any other person, in any way whatsoever. That is completely at odds and would place you squarely in disharmony with Universal Intelligence. There is not the slightest necessity for doing so; indeed, any attempt to use your will upon others will only lead to defeating your purpose.

Universal Intelligent Thinking Substance is friendly to you, and it is more anxious to give you what you want than you are to get it.

To succeed and Manifest your Best-Life, you need only to use your willpower upon yourself.

When you know what to think and do, then you must use your will to compel yourself to think and do the right things. That is the legitimate use of the will in getting what you want—to use it in holding yourself to the right course. Use *your will* to keep yourself thinking and acting in the Universal Way.

Use your mind to form a clear mental image of what you want, and hold that vision with Faith and purpose. Use *your will* to keep your mind working in the Universal Way.

The steadier and more continuous your Faith and purpose, the more rapidly you will succeed, Manifest your Best-Life, and enjoy happiness because you will make only *positive* impressions upon Universal Intelligent Original Thinking Substance. And you will not neutralize or offset them by negative impressions.

The picture of your desires, held with Faith and purpose, is taken up by the Universal Intelligent Thinking Substance, which permeates it to great distances throughout the Universe.

As your impression spreads, all things are set moving toward your realization. Every living thing, every inanimate thing, and things yet uncreated, are stirred toward bringing into being that which you want. All force begins to be exerted in your direction. All things begin to move toward you. The minds of people, everywhere, are influenced toward doing the things necessary to the fulfillment of your desires. And they work for you, unconsciously and approvingly.

But you can check all this by starting a negative impression in the Universal Formless Substance. Doubt or unbelief are as certain to start a movement away from you as Faith and purpose are to start one toward you. It is by not understanding this that most people who try to make use of "mental science" to succeed make their failure. Every hour and moment you spend in giving heed to doubts and fears, every hour you spend in worry, every hour in which your Spirit is possessed by unbelief sets a current away from you in the whole domain of Universal Intelligent Substance.

All of Universal Intelligence's promises are unto you who Believe and have Faith, and unto you only.

Universal Intelligence is insistent upon this point of Belief and Faith, and now you know the reason why.

Since Belief and Faith are all important, it behooves you to guard your thoughts. And as your Beliefs and Faith may be shaped to a very great extent by the things you observe and think about, it is important that you should *vigilantly* command and direct your attention.

And it is here that *your will* comes into use, for it is by your will that you determine upon what things your attention shall be fixed.

You are to immediately "cancel" or "reject" any negative suggestion made into your Subconscious Mind by you, another person, or any other source.

"I cancel and affirm the opposite."

"I reject…"

Things are not brought into being by thinking about their opposites. Health is never to be attained by studying disease and thinking about disease. Righteousness is not to be promoted by studying sin and thinking about sin. And no one ever improved their wealth by studying poverty and thinking about poverty.

And you cannot hold the mental image that is to create your success if you fill your mind with pictures of poverty. Do not read anything that fills your mind with gloomy images of want and suffering.

What tends to do away with poverty is not getting pictures of poverty into the minds of those who are wealthy but rather getting pictures of success and wealth into the minds of those who are in poverty.

Your focus should be on the true cure.

Poverty can be done away with, not by increasing the number of well-to-do people who think about poverty, but by increasing the number of poor people who propose with Faith to succeed and live their Best-Life.

What the poor truly need are living examples, social proof, leadership, *hope*, and inspiration.

Charity only sends them a loaf of bread to keep them alive in their current environment, or gives them entertainment to make them forget for an hour or two. But inspiration will cause them to rise out of their situation. If you want to help the poor, demonstrate to them that they can succeed. Prove it by your success and then they will know from your example what you speak about when you reach out to help them.

Give a fish... you have given a meal... teach to fish... you have fed for a lifetime.

The only way in which poverty will ever be banished from this world is by getting a large and constantly increasing number of people to practice the teachings of this book.

People must be taught to succeed and Manifest their Best-Life by creation, not by competition.

Every person who succeeds by competition throws down behind them the ladder by which they rise and keeps others down. But every person who succeeds by creation opens a way for thousands, or even millions, to follow them, and greatly inspires them to do so.

Chapter 10:

Further Use of Your Will To Manifest Your Goal

"Change your conception of yourself and you will automatically change the world in which you live. Do not try to change people; they are only messengers telling you who you are. Revalue yourself and they will confirm the change."
—Neville Goddard

"Your habits will make you or break you as in this Universe it is always only 'you vs. you.' You are your only problem, and you are your only solution. All you have is today. There is no past. There is no future. All you have is the present. Cherish it. Always think and act in the present. Universal Intelligence only operates, works, and communicates in the present."
—P. J. DiNuzzo

Y ou cannot retain a true and clear vision of success and Manifesting your Best-Life if you are constantly turning your attention to opposing pictures, whether they be external or imaginary.

Do not tell of your past troubles of a financial nature. If you have had them, do not think of them at all. Do not dwell on and tell of the poverty of your parents, or grandparents, or the hardships of your early life. To do any of these things is to mentally class yourself with the poor for the time being. And it will certainly reduce the likelihood of you Manifesting positive outcomes.

If you are constantly complaining about your upbringing, stop it immediately, for it is not your mother's, father's, grandparents', or any other of your relatives' fault.

All you have is today.

There is no past. There is no future. All you have is the present. Cherish it.

Always think and act in the present.

Universal Intelligence only operates, works, and communicates *in the present.*

By dwelling on anything from the past, you are completely out of harmony with Universal Intelligence and will *never* Manifest your goal while on this frequency and vibration.

When any negative thoughts of your upbringing arise, *immediately* state, "he/she/they did the best that they could." *And move on.*

Always remember, whatever you think, your thoughts, is what you attract.

If your thoughts are positive, *you will attract more positive.*

If your thoughts are negative, *you will attract more negative.*

You have been given and hold the Universal Keys to happiness in your mind. Use them wisely.

Put poverty and all things that pertain to poverty completely behind you.

To succeed, you must accept the Core Theory of Universal Intelligence as being correct. You must rest all your hopes to *Manifest Anything You Can Imagine* on Its being correct. What can you gain by giving heed to negative or conflicting theories?

Do not read books that tell you that the world is soon coming to an end. And do not read the writings of muck-rakers and pessimistic philosophers who tell you of its future collapse.

The world is not on its way to ending; quite the contrary, it is expressing, expanding, increasing, and growing.

It is a wonderful, wonderful, wonderful Becoming of Life.

True, there may be a good many things in existing conditions that are disagreeable, but what is the use of studying them when they are certainly passing away, and when the study of them only tends to check their passing and keep them with us? Why give time and attention to things that are being removed by evolutionary improvement and growth, when you can hasten their removal only by promoting the evolutionary growth as far as your part of it goes?

No matter how horrible the conditions may seem to be in certain countries, sections, or places, you waste your time and destroy your own chances by considering and dwelling on them.

You should rather interest yourself in helping your fellow brothers and sisters, and advancing both them and the world.

Think of the success the world is coming into instead of the poverty it is growing out of, and bear in your Mind that the only way in which you can assist the world toward success is by yourself succeeding *through the creative method—not the competitive one.*

Give your attention wholly to Manifesting success, health, wealth, relationships, happiness, Gratitude, and your goal.

Whenever you think or speak of those who are poor, think and speak of them as those who can start on their pathway to success, as those who are to be congratulated rather than pitied. Then they and others can follow your lead, catch the inspiration, and begin to search for their way out.

Because I say that you are to give your whole time and Mind and thought to Manifesting your Best-Life, it does not follow that you are ever to be sordid or mean.

To become truly successful in your health, wealth, and happiness is the noblest aim you can have in life, for it includes everything else.

On the competitive plane, the struggle to succeed is a vain scramble for power over other men and women. But when we come into the creative mind, all this is changed.

All that is possible in the way of greatness and Spirit Unfoldment, of service and lofty endeavor, comes by way of Manifesting and being successful. All is made possible by the use of things.

If you have no tools, you cannot build.

If you lack physical health, you will find that the attainment of it is conditional on your success in Manifesting.

Those who are emancipated from financial worry, and who have the means to live a carefree existence and follow hygienic practices, can have and retain health.

Moral and Spiritual greatness are possible only to those who are above the competitive battle for existence. And only those who are succeeding on the plane of creative thought are free from the degrading influences of competition. If your heart is set on domestic happiness, remember that love flourishes best where there is refinement, a high level of thought, and freedom from corrupting influences. And these are to be found only where success is attained by the exercise of creative thought, without strife or rivalry.

You can aim at nothing so great or noble, I repeat, as to succeed and to help and inspire your fellow brothers and sisters. And you must fix your attention upon your mental picture of your thought-form and Manifesting to the exclusion of all that may tend to dim or obscure your vision and purpose.

You must learn to see the true underlying UNIVERSAL TRUTH in all things. You must see beneath all seemingly wrong conditions and know that Universal Intelligence is ever moving forward toward *fuller expression* and more complete happiness and has a desire for you to Co-Create with It and do so as well.

Take the leap. Jump on board with me and hitch a ride, the greatest ride of your life.

It is Universal Intelligence's TRUTH that there is no such thing as poverty, that there is only abundance.

It is Universal Intelligence's TRUTH that there is no such thing as illness, that there is only health.

Some people remain in poverty because they are ignorant of the fact that there is wealth available for them, and these people can best be taught by showing them the way to "social proof" Success in your own person and practice, through setting an example they can follow.

For others, the very best thing you can do is to arouse their desire by showing them the happiness that comes from Manifesting your goal. Demonstrate success to them.

Others still are poor because, while they have some notion of Universal Science, they have become so swamped and lost in the maze of metaphysical and occult theories that they do not know which road to take. They try a mixture of many systems and fail in all. For these people, again, the very best thing to do is to show them the right way in your own person and practice.

An ounce of doing things is worth a pound of theorizing.

Again, *the* very best thing you can do for the whole world is to succeed and make the most of yourself.

You can serve Universal Intelligence and your fellow brothers and sisters in no more effective way than by succeeding; that is, if you enjoy your Best-Life by the creative method, and not by the competitive one.

Another thing I assert that my book, and my websites give in detail, are the principles of the Universal Way, Universal Laws, and the Universal Science of Manifesting. And if this is true, you do not need to read any other book on the subject. This may sound narrow and egotistical, but consider that there is no more scientific method of computation in mathematics than by addition, subtraction, multiplication, and division.

No other method is possible.

There can be but one shortest distance between two points. There is only one way to think scientifically, and that is to think in the way that leads by the most direct and simple route to your goal. No one has yet formulated a briefer or less complex "system" than the one I have set forth herein. It has been stripped of all nonessentials. When you commence this, lay all others aside. Put them out of your mind altogether.

Read my book every day. Read at least one page every day.

My book will lead and guide you to *Manifest Anything You Can Imagine*.

Keep it with you, commit it to memory, and do not think about other "systems" and "theories." If you do, you will begin to have doubts and be confused, and you will be uncertain and wavering in your thought, and then you will begin to falter and fail.

After you have learned to Manifest success and positive results, you may study other systems as much as you please. But until you are absolutely positive on how to Manifest your goal, dreams, and wishes and you have gained what you want, do not read anything on this line but my book.

Read only the most optimistic comments on the world's news, those in harmony with your thought-form and TRUTH.

Now, this and the preceding chapters have brought you and I to my following statement of Universal Intelligence's basic facts:

There is a Universal Intelligent Original Thinking Substance from which all things are made, and which, in Its original state, permeates, penetrates, and fills the interspaces of the entire Universe.

Your Thought in this Substance produces the Thought-Form and thing that you Image by your Thought.

You can Form things in your Thought, and by impressing your Thought-Form upon Universal Intelligent Thinking Substance, you can cause the thing you Think about to be Created.

In order to do this, you must pass from the Competitive to the Creative Mind. You must Form a clear Mental Picture and Thought-Form of the Goal and thing you Want. Hold this Picture in your Thoughts and in your Mind with a Burning-Desire and fixed PURPOSE to get what you Want and the unwavering FAITH that you do get what you Want, closing your Mind against all that may tend to shake your Purpose, dim your Vision, or squelch your Faith.

And in addition to all this, you shall now see that in order to Manifest you must live, think, and act in the Universal Way.

Chapter 11:

Acting in the Universal Way... "Action" Is the Key to Completing the "Physical-Back" of Your Goal

"If you see it in your mind, you will hold it in your hand."
—Bob Proctor

"Close your eyes, and in your mind, imagine a beautiful green natural grass football field. Focus on the middle of the field in front of you, as this is where you will produce with your thoughts and meet with your actions your Manifested goal. Imagine yourself standing at one goal line staring the entire length of the field at the distant goal or goal line. Your thought creates and delivers your goal toward you to midfield. Your action produces results that allow you to walk toward and meet your thought-form at midfield, allowing you to physically accept, grab, and embrace your goal."
—P. J. DiNuzzo

A *ll Manifesting starts with thought,* for it is the creative power, or the force that initiates and causes the Universal Creative Power to act.

Thinking in the Universal Way will bring success, happiness, and your Best-Life to you, but you must not rely upon thought alone, paying no attention to *personal action.* For this is the rock upon which many otherwise scientific metaphysical thinkers meet shipwreck—*the failure to connect thought with personal action.*

Close your eyes, and in your mind, imagine a beautiful green natural grass football field, in the US or Internationally. Focus on the middle of the field in front of you, as this is where you will produce with your thoughts and meet with your actions your Manifested goal. Imagine yourself standing at one goal staring the entire length of the field at the distant goal or goal line. Your *thought creates* and delivers your goal toward you to midfield. Your *action* produces results that allow you to walk toward and meet your thought-form at midfield, allowing you to *physically* accept, grab, and embrace your goal.

Any *action* you take starts with you making a *decision.* Learn to make your decisions quickly and to change them slowly if you change them at all. Learn to get in tune with your Subconscious Mind, which is connected directly to Universal Intelligence and the Universal Subconscious Mind. *Your Subconscious Mind is connected to all information from all time* and is dying to give you and provide you with the correct answer or solution *every* single time you need it. Learn to differentiate what your Conscious Mind is telling you from the golden advice and direction your Subconscious Mind is providing. My Subconscious Mind, in a very soft unspoken tone and message, provides me with the answer and gives me one or maybe two seconds to recognize it and act on it. The longer you wait, the worse it is for your decision-making success as your *"paradigm"* starts to take over and typically provides a hundred reasons why you should not take action. For this reason,

Andrew Carnegie would not hire a manager if they could not make a difficult decision within approximately less than thirty seconds because he knew the poor quality of decisions that are made by your paradigm when you procrastinate.

Humankind has not yet reached the stage of development, even supposing such a stage to be possible, in which you can create directly from Universal Formless Substance without action and nature's processes or the work of human hands. You must not only think, but your personal action *must* also supplement your thought.

Earlier in my book I strongly recommended watching *The Secret* movie, but please do so with one key note of caution. The movie does not emphasize clearly enough the importance of taking the proper level of *action* in order to Manifest your goal.

By thought you can cause the gold in the hearts of the mountains to be impelled toward you, but it will not mine itself, refine itself, coin itself, and come rolling down the highway seeking its way into your pocket.

Under the impelling power of Universal Intelligence, your affairs will be so ordered that someone will be led to mine the gold for you. Other people's business transactions will be so directed that the gold will be brought toward you, and you must arrange your own business affairs so that you will be able to receive it when it comes to you. Your thought makes and creates all things, animate and inanimate, and works to bring you what you want, but your personal activities and actions must be such that you can rightly receive what you want when it reaches you.

Always remember, the key equation in order to be in harmony with Universal Intelligence and successfully Manifest is that *you must provide every man and woman more in Use Value than they give you in Cash Value.*

The Universal Scientific use of thought consists in forming a clear and distinct mental image and thought-form of what you want, in holding fast to the purpose to get what you want, and in realizing with Grateful Faith that you *do* get what you want.

The action of thought in succeeding is fully explained in my preceding chapters. Your Faith and purpose positively impress your vision and goal upon Universal Intelligent Formless Substance, which has THE SAME (OR GREATER) DESIRE FOR MORE LIFE THAT YOU HAVE, and this vision and goal, received from you, sets all the Universal Creative forces at work, *in and through their regular channels of action* but directed toward you.

It is not your part to guide or supervise the creative process. All you have to do with that is to retain your vision, stick to your purpose, and maintain your burning-desire, Faith, and Gratitude.

You are *never* to ask or think about *"if," "how," or "when"* when Manifesting your goal.

"I AM So Happy and Grateful Now That I never ask, if, how, or when."

"I AM So Happy and Grateful Now That I achieve every goal I set with fun, effortlessly and easily."

But you must act in the Universal Way and in harmony with the Universal Laws, so that you can receive what is yours when it comes to you, so that you can meet the things you have in your picture and put them in their proper places as they arrive.

You can readily see the TRUTH of this.

When things reach you, they will be in the hands of other men and women, who will ask an equivalent value for them, which you will be happy to provide.

You can only get what is yours by giving the other person what is theirs.

Your pocketbook is not going to be transformed into a Fortunatus's purse, which shall always be full of money and gold every morning when you awaken, without any effort on your part.

Remember, your *actions* must meet what your *thoughts* have created for you to Manifest and then physically grab, embrace, and enjoy your goal.

This is the crucial point in the Universal Science of Manifesting your Goal, right here, where Thought and personal Action must be combined and where they meet.

There are very many people who, Consciously or Unconsciously, set the creative forces in action by the strength and persistence of their desires, but who remain poor because they do not provide proper actions for the reception of the thing they want when it comes.

By thought, the goal you both want and have a burning-desire for is brought to you; *by action* you meet it, accept it, grab it, and receive it.

Whatever your action is to be, it is of mission critical importance that you must act *now*. You cannot act in the past, and it is essential to the clearness of your mental vision that you *dismiss the past from your mind*. You cannot act in the future, for the future is not here yet. And you cannot tell how you will want to act in any future contingency until that contingency has arrived.

The past is history... the future is a mystery... but today... today is a gift... that is why it is called "the present."

Because you are not in the right business, job, career, or environment now, do not think that you must postpone action until you get into the right business, job, career, or environment. And do not spend time in the present taking thought as to the best course in possible future emergencies. Have Faith in your ability to meet any emergency when it arrives.

If you act in the present with your mind on the future, your present action will be with a divided mind and will not be effective. It will never work.

ALL YOU HAVE IS THE PRESENT, and what you will be able to Manifest and accomplish in the present will be beyond your wildest dreams.

To *Manifest Anything You Can Imagine*, put your whole mind, body, heart, Spirit, and emotions into *present* action.

Do not give your creative impulse to Universal Intelligent Thinking Substance, and then sit down and wait for results. If you do, you will never get them.

Act now.

THERE IS NEVER ANY TIME BUT NOW, AND THERE WILL NEVER BE ANY TIME BUT NOW.

There is no such thing as time or distance in the Universe.

If you are ever to begin to be ready for the reception of what you want, you must begin *now.*

And your action, whatever it is, must most likely be in your present business or employment, and it must be upon the persons and things in your present environment.

You cannot act where you are not, you cannot act where you have been, and you cannot act where you are going to be; *you can act only where you are... NOW.*

Do not bother thinking about whether yesterday's work was well done or ill done; *do today's work well.*

Do not try to do tomorrow's work now. There will be plenty of time to do that when you get to it.

Do not try, by occult or mystical means, to act on people or things that are out of your reach.

Do not wait for a change of environment before you act. Get a change of environment by action.

Believe in me, that you can act upon the environment in which you are now so as to cause yourself to be transferred to a better environment.

Always hold with Faith and purpose the vision of yourself in the better environment, but act upon your present environment with all your heart, with all your strength, with all your emotion, and with all your mind.

Do not spend any time daydreaming or castle building. Hold to the one vision of your goal of what you want and act *now*.

Do not cast about seeking some new thing to do, or some strange, unusual, or remarkable action to perform as a first step toward Manifesting your goal. It is probable that your actions, at least for some time to come, will be those you have been performing for some time past, but you are to begin now to perform these actions in the Universal Way, which will surely lead you to success.

If you are engaged in some business, job, or career, and you feel that it is not the right one for you, *do not wait* until you get into the right business, job, or career before you begin to act.

Do not feel discouraged, or sit down and lament because you are misplaced. No person was ever so misplaced that they could not find the right place, and no person ever became so involved in the wrong business, job, or career that they could not get into the right business, job, or career.

Hold the vision of yourself in the right business, with the purpose to get into it and the Faith that you will get into it and are getting into it, but *act* in your present place. Use your present place as the quickest means of getting to a better one. Your vision of the right business, job, or career, if held with Faith and purpose, will cause Universal Intelligence to move the right result toward you, and your action, if performed in the Universal Way, will cause you to move toward success.

If you are an employee, or wage earner, and feel that you must change places in order to get what you want, do not "project" your thought into space and rely upon it to get you another job. It will probably fail to do so.

Hold the vision and goal of yourself in the job you want, while you *act* with Faith and purpose on the job you have, and you will certainly get the job you want.

Your vision, goal, and Faith will set the *creative forces* in motion to bring it toward you, and your action will cause the forces in *your own environment* to move you toward the place you want. In closing this chapter, I will add another statement to our syllabus:

There is a Universal Intelligence Original Thinking Substance from which all things are made, and which, in Its original state, permeates, penetrates, and fills the interspaces of the entire Universe.

Your Thought in this Substance produces the Thought-Form and thing that you Image in your Thought.

You can Form things in your Thought, and by impressing your Thought-Form with Emotion and a Burning-Desire upon Universal Original Thinking Substance, you can cause the thing you Think about to be Created.

In order to do this, you must pass from the Competitive to the Creative Mind, you must Form a clear Mental Picture and Thought-Form of the Goal and thing you Want, and you must hold this Picture in your Thought and in your Mind with the fixed PURPOSE of getting what you Want and the unwavering FAITH that you do get what you Want, closing your Mind to all that may tend to shake your Purpose, dim your Vision, or squelch your Faith.

That you may receive what you Want when it comes, you must Act now upon the people and things in your present environment.

Chapter 12:

"Efficient Action"... to Meet Your Thoughts and Grab, Embrace, and Enjoy Your Manifested Goal

"The Law of Attraction states that whatever you focus on, think about, read about, and talk about intensely, you're going to attract more of it into your life."
— Jack Canfield

"You must get out of your current comfort zone in order to succeed. No one has ever had an improvement, breakthrough, 'Quantum Leap,' or ever Manifested their goal, while gliding through life and languishing in their comfort zone. A burning-desire and emotions are the yeast that raise the dough."
—P. J. DiNuzzo

You must use your thought, directly support it with emotion as I directed in previous chapters, and begin to do what you can do where you are, and you must do *all* that you can do where you are.

You can advance *only by being larger* than your present place, and no person is larger than their present place who leaves undone any of the work pertaining to that place.

The world is advanced only by those who more than fill their present places.

You must get out of your current *comfort zone* in order to succeed.

No one has ever had an improvement, breakthrough, or "Quantum Leap", or ever Manifested their goal, while gliding through life and languishing in their *comfort zone*.

You can only glide in one direction, downward, and that direction is certainly not in harmony with growth and Universal Intelligence.

If you continue to do exactly what you have always done, you will continue to receive exactly what you have always received with no improvement.

If no person quite filled their present place, you can see that there must be a going backward in everything. The progress of the world is slowed only by those who do not fill the places they are holding. No society could advance if every person was smaller than their place. Social evolution is guided by the law of physical and mental evolution. In the animal world, evolution is caused by excess of life.

When an organism has more life than can be expressed in the functions of its own plane, it develops the organs of a higher plane, and a new species is originated.

There never would have been new species had there not been organisms that more than filled their places. The Universal Law is exactly the same for you. You Manifesting, succeeding, and enjoying your Best-Life depends upon you applying this Universal Principle to your own affairs.

Every day is either a successful day or a day of failure, and it is the successful days that get you what you want. If every day is a failure, you can never succeed, while if every day is a success, you cannot fail.

If there is something that may be done today, and you do not do it, you have failed in so far as that thing is concerned, and the consequences may be more disastrous than you imagine.

You cannot foresee the results of even the most trivial act, for you do not know the workings and movement of all the Universal Subconscious Mind forces that have been set moving on your behalf. Much may depend on your doing some simple act, and it may be the very thing that will open the door of opportunity to very great possibilities. You can never know all the combinations that Universal Intelligence is making for you in the world of things and of human affairs. Your neglect or failure to do some seemingly small thing may cause a long delay in the Manifestation of your goal and getting what you want.

Do, every day, *all* that can be done that day.

There is, however, a limitation or qualification to the above that you must take in to account.

You are not to overwork, nor to rush blindly into your business in an effort to do the greatest possible number of things in the shortest possible time.

You are not to try to do tomorrow's work today, nor to do a week's work in a day.

When I AM coaching you, you will hear me use the word "TMIT" (Three Most Important Tasks) or "SMIT" (Six Most Important Tasks) a lot. In order for you to *Manifest Anything You Can Imagine*, you must more than fill your present space by performing action, specifically efficient action. Your daily efficient action should be a minimum of your TMIT and a maximum of your SMIT. Once you are in harmony with your daily ritual, your Subconscious Mind will let you know what these actions are. It will be obvious to you what your most important tasks are that you get to do each day when you perform your "evening preview" the night before. Your TMIT are the actions that will make the biggest impact toward your goal and your Best-Life and require your focus, discipline, and effort.

It is not really the number of things you do, but the *efficiency* of each separate *action* that counts.

Every act is, in itself, either a success or a failure.

Every act is, in itself, either effective or ineffective, efficient or inefficient.

Every inefficient act is a failure, and if you spend your life in doing inefficient acts, your whole life will be a failure.

The more things you do, the worse for you if all your acts are inefficient ones.

On the other hand, every efficient act is a success in itself, and if every act of your life is an efficient one, your whole life *must* be a success.

Regarding action, the cause of failure is doing too many things in an inefficient manner, and not doing enough things in an efficient manner.

You will see that it is a self-evident proposition that if you do not do any inefficient acts, and if you do a sufficient number of efficient acts, you will succeed. If, now, it is possible for you to make each act an efficient one, you see again that achieving success by Co-Creating with Universal Intelligence is reduced to an *exact science*, like mathematics.

The matter turns, then, to the question of whether you can make each separate action a success in itself. And this you can certainly do.

You can make each action a success because your Spiritual Spark, Spiritual DNA, and Spirit are Perfect, *and* Universal Power desires for your success and is working with you constantly, and Universal Power cannot fail.

Universal Power is at your service to Co-Create with you to Manifest, achieve, and grab your dreams, wishes, and goal, and to make each action efficient, you have only to put *focus*, *discipline*, *effort*, and *emotion* into it.

Every action is either strong or weak, and when every action is strong, you are acting in the Universal Way, which will cause you to succeed.

Every act can be made strong and efficient by holding your vision and goal with a burning-desire while you are doing it and putting the whole power of your FAITH, GRATITUDE, and PURPOSE into it.

It is at this point that the people who separate mental power from personal action fail. They use the power of mind in one place and at one time, and they act in another place and at another time, creating a "double-binding message." Since their acts are not successful in themselves, too many of them are inefficient. But if Universal Power goes into every act, no matter how commonplace, every act will be a success in itself, and as in the nature of things, every success opens the way to other successes, you progress toward what you want, and the progress of what you want toward you will become increasingly rapid.

Your future excites me beyond words.

Put momentum on your side and ride the *current of energy and flow* with the Universal Way.

Remember that successful action is cumulative in its results. This is how you generate your Quantum Leap. Since the desire for more life is inherent in all things, when you begin to move toward larger life, more good things attract themselves to you, and the influence of your desire is multiplied.

Do, every day, all that you can do that day, and do each action in an efficient manner.

In saying that you must hold your vision and goal while you are doing each action with emotion, however trivial or commonplace, I do not mean to say that it is necessary at all times to see the vision and goal distinctly to its smallest details. It should be the work of your leisure hours to use your imagination and visualization on the details of your vision and goal and to contemplate them with a burning-desire until they are firmly fixed upon your memory.

If you wish for speedy results, spend practically all your spare time on this practice.

By "spaced-repetition" and continuous contemplation with a burning-desire, you will get the picture of what you want, even to the smallest details, so firmly fixed upon your mind, and so completely transferred to the mind of Universal Original Thinking Substance, that in your working hours you need only to mentally refer to the picture of your goal to stimulate your Faith and purpose and cause your best effort to be put forth. Contemplate your goal's picture in your leisure hours until your Consciousness is so full of it that you can grasp and emotionalize it instantly. You will become so enthused with its bright promises that the mere thought of it will call forth the strongest emotion and energies of your whole being.

Let me again repeat our syllabus, and by slightly changing the closing statements, bring it to the point you and I have now reached.

There is a Universal Intelligence Original Thinking Substance from which all things are made, and which, in Its original state, permeates, penetrates, and fills the interspaces of the entire Universe.

Your Thought in this Original Substance produces the Thought-Form and thing that you Image by your Thought.

You can Form things in your Thought, and by impressing your Thought-Form with Emotion upon Universal Intelligence Thinking Substance, you can cause the thing you Think about to be Created.

In order to do this, you must pass from the Competitive to the Creative Mind, you must Form a clear Mental Picture of the thing and Goal you Want, and do, with Faith and Purpose, all that can be done each day, doing each separate Action in an efficient manner.

Chapter 13:

Getting into the
Right Business, Job, or Career

"I am no longer cursed by poverty because I took possession of my own mind, and that mind has yielded me every material thing I want, and much more than I need. But this power of mind is a universal one, available to the humblest person as it is to the greatest."
—Andrew Carnegie

"Most people are thinking about what they don't want, and they're wondering why it shows up over and over again."
—John Assaraf

"Never forget: Your Spiritual Spark is Perfect. Your Spiritual DNA is Perfect. Your Spirit is Perfect. And you are a magnet and attract toward you the exact type of energy that you put out into the Universe. Therefore… I AM. I AM. I AM. I AM."
—P. J. DiNuzzo

Success, in any particular business, job, or career, depends for one thing upon your possessing in a well-developed state the ability required to succeed.

Without good musical ability, no one can succeed as a teacher of music. Without well-developed mechanical abilities, no one can achieve great success in any of the mechanical trades. Without tact and commercial abilities, no one can succeed in business and entrepreneurial pursuits. But to possess in a well-developed state the abilities required in your particular vocation does not ensure success. There are musicians who have remarkable talent who remain poor. There are electricians, carpenters, plumbers, and so on who have excellent mechanical ability who do not succeed, and there are merchants and entrepreneurs with good abilities for dealing with men and women who nevertheless fail.

The different abilities are tools. It is essential to have good tools, but it is also essential that the tools are used in the Universal Way. One person can take a sharp saw, a square, a good plane, and so on, and build a beautiful article of furniture. Another person can take the same tools and set to work to duplicate the article, but their production will be a disaster. For they do not know how to use good tools in a successful way.

The various abilities of your mind are the tools with which you must do the work as it will be easier for you to succeed if you get into a business for which you are well equipped with mental tools.

Generally speaking, you will do best in the business that will use your strongest abilities, the one for which you are naturally "best fitted." But there are limitations to this statement also. No person should regard their employment situation as being irrevocably fixed by the tendencies with which they were born.

You can succeed in *any* career, job, or business, for if you have not the right talent for it you can develop that talent. It merely means that you will have to make your tools as you go along, instead of confining yourself to the use of those with which you were born. It will be *easier* for you to succeed in a position for which you already have the talents in a well-developed state, but you *can* succeed in any vocation, for you can develop any rudimentary talent, and there is no talent of which you have not at least the rudiment.

You will succeed and manifest most easily in point of effort if you do that for which you are best fitted, but you will succeed most satisfactorily if you do that which you *want* to do.

Doing what you want to do is life, and there is no real satisfaction in living if we are compelled to be forever doing something we do not like to do and can never do what we want to do. And it is certain that you can do what you want to do. The desire to do it is proof that you have within you the power that can do it.

Follow your bliss.

Desire is a Manifestation of power.

Desire is the effort of an unexpressed possibility within seeking expression without through your action.

A burning-desire and emotions are the yeast that raise the dough.

The desire to play music is the power that can play music seeking expression and development. The desire to invent mechanical devices is the mechanical talent seeking expression and development.

Where there is no power, either developed or undeveloped, to do a thing, there is never any desire to do that thing, and where there is strong desire to do a thing, it is certain proof that the power to do it is strong, and it only requires to be developed and applied in the Universal Way.

All else being equal, it is best to select the business for which you have the best developed ability and talent, but if you have a strong desire to engage in any particular line of work, you should select that work as the ultimate end at which you aim.

You can do what you want to do, and it is your right and privilege to follow the business, job, or career that will be most pleasant for you.

You are not obliged to do what you do not like to do, and you should not do it except as a means to bring you to the doing of the thing you want to do.

If there are past mistakes whose consequences have placed you in an undesirable career, job, business, or environment, you may be obliged for some time to do what you do not like to do, but you can make the doing of it pleasant by knowing that it is making it possible for you to get closer to what you want to do. If you feel that you are not in the right vocation, do not act too hastily in trying to get into another one.

The best way, generally, to change your career, job, business, or environment is by growth and to *start from where you are currently at today.*

Do not be afraid to make a sudden and radical change if your intuition is favorable and the opportunity is presented, and you feel after consideration that it is the right opportunity, but never take sudden or radical action when your intuition is in doubt as to the wisdom of doing so.

There is never any hurry or lack of opportunity on the creative plane.

When you get out of your competitive mind, you will understand that you never need to act hastily. No one else is going to beat you to the thing you want to do; there is enough for all.

There is abundance everywhere in the Universe.

If one place is taken, another better one will be opened for you a little further on, there is plenty of time. When you are in doubt, wait. Fall back on the contemplation of your vision, goal, and imagination, and increase your Faith, emotion, and purpose, and by all means, in times of doubt and indecision, cultivate your Gratitude.

A day or two spent contemplating your Faith, purpose, goal, and burning-desire of what you want, and in earnest appreciation and Gratitude that you are getting it, will bring your mind into such close relationship with Universal Intelligence that you will make no mistake when you do act.

There is a Universal Subconscious Mind that *your* Perfect Spiritual Spark, Perfect Spirit, and Perfect Spiritual DNA are directly connected to inside of you that possesses all knowledge of all time, and you can come into closer and closer unity with this Universal Mind by Faith and the purpose of advancing in life if you have and maintain deep Gratitude.

Mistakes come from acting hastily, or from acting in fear or doubt, or in forgetfulness of the Universal Motive, which is *More Life to All, and Less Life to None.*

As you go on in the Universal Way, opportunities will come to you in increasing number, and you will need to be very steady in your Faith and purpose and keep in close touch with the Universal Mind by reverent Gratitude.

Do all that you can do with your best effort every day, but do it without haste, hurry, rush, worry, or fear.

Go as fast as you can, but never hurry.

Go as fast as you can, but never rush.

Remember that in the moment you begin to hurry, you cease to be a creator and become a competitor. You drop back onto the old competitive plane again.

Whenever you find yourself hurrying, call a halt, fix your attention on the mental image of the thing you want, and begin to give thanks that you are getting it.

Your exercise of GRATITUDE will *never* fail to strengthen your Faith and renew your purpose.

Chapter 19:
Delivering Your "Impression of Increase" to Your Fellow Brothers and Sisters

"Everything is energy and that's all there is to it.
Match the frequency of the reality you want
and you cannot help but get that reality.
It can be no other way.
This is not philosophy.
This is physics."
—Albert Einstein

"Always remember, the key to being in harmony with Universal
Intelligence and successfully Manifest is that you should always
strive to provide your fellow brothers and sisters with the
'Impression of Increase' and deliver a Use Value that is higher than
the Cash Value you receive from them."
—P. J. DiNuzzo

W hether you change your work environment or not, your actions for the present should be those pertaining to the business, job, or career in which you are *now* engaged.

You can get into the future line of work you want by making constructive use of the business you are already established in, by doing your daily work in an efficient manner and growing in the Universal Way.

And in so far as your current line of work consists of dealing with other people, whether in person or virtually, the key thought of all your efforts must be to convey to their minds your *impression of increase.*

Increase, expression, expansion, growth, and happiness are what all men and all women are seeking. It is the primal urge of the Universal Original Formless Thinking Intelligence within them, seeking fuller increase and more life.

The desire for increase is inherent in all nature. It is the fundamental impulse of the Universe and Universal Intelligence. All human activities are based on the desire for increase. People are seeking more food, more clothes, better shelter, more luxury, more beauty, better companionship, more knowledge, more pleasure—increase in something equals more life.

It is not greed, so never be self-conscious. This is how the Universe was created by Universal Intelligence and designed specifically for you and to *co-create* with you.

Remember, your mind is a center of divine operation.

The Universe is a perfect and infinite sea of wisdom, love, life, abundance, joy, and harmony.

Universal Intelligence has set your table in front of you for you to express, expand, increase, grow, succeed, Manifest, and fulfill your dreams and wishes by living your Best-Life. Step into your new 1 percent better self every single morning and co-create with It. This is Universal Intelligence's primal desire for you.

Every living thing is under this necessity for continuous Advancement. Where Increase of Life ceases, dissolution and death set in at once.

You instinctively know this, and thus you are and should forever be seeking more and to be in harmony with this Universal Truth.

This is the Universal Law of Perpetual Increase and Motion.

The normal desire for increased wealth is not an evil or a reprehensible thing. It is in harmony with the Universe and is simply the desire for a more abundant life. *It is pure aspiration.*

And because it is the deepest instinct of our natures, all men and women are attracted to others who can give them more of the means of life.

In following the Universal Way as I have described in my foregoing pages, you are getting continuous increase for yourself, and you are giving it to all with whom you deal.

You are a purposely designed creative center, custom crafted by Universal Intelligence, from which increase is given off to all.

Be sure of this, and convey assurance of this fact to every man, woman, and child with whom you come in contact. No matter how small the transaction, even if it is only the selling of a stick of candy to a young child, put into it the thought and impression of increase, and make sure that the customer or client is rightfully impressed with your thought.

Convey the impression of Advancement with everything you do so that all people shall receive the Impression that you are an *advancing person*, and that you advance all who deal with you. Even to the people whom you meet in a social way, without any thought of business, and to whom you do not try to sell anything, give and deliver this thought and impression of increase.

You can convey this impression by holding the unshakable Faith that you, yourself, are in the way of increase, and by letting this Faith inspire, fill, and permeate every action you perform.

Let it naturally flow out of every pore of your body with the *highest vibration.*

Do everything that you do in the firm conviction *that you are an advancing personality*, and that you are giving advancement to everyone you interact with.

Feel that you are succeeding, have accomplished your goal, and that in so doing, you are making others successful and conferring benefits on all with whom you come into contact, in business, your personal life, or otherwise.

Do not boast or brag of your success or talk about it unnecessarily.

Remain humble, yet confident, at all times.

True Faith is never boastful.

Wherever you find a boastful person, you find one who is secretly doubtful and afraid. Simply feel the Faith, and let it work out in every transaction. Let every act and tone and look express the quiet assurance that you are successful. Words will not be necessary to communicate this feeling to others. They will feel your vibration and sense of increase when in your presence and will be attracted to you again.

You must impress others so much that they will feel that by associating with you, they will get increase for themselves.

Remember Universal Intelligence's Ethos: always give and deliver unto others a *use value* greater than the *cash value* you are receiving from them.

Take an honest pride in doing this, and let everybody know it, and you will have no lack of customers, clients, or friends. People will go where they are given increase, and Universal Intelligence, which desires increase in all, and which knows all, will move toward you and men and women who have never heard of you. Your business will increase rapidly, and you will be surprised at the unexpected benefits that will come to you. You will be able from day to day to make larger combinations, secure greater advantages, and go into a more desirable business, career, or job if you so desire.

But in doing all this, you must never lose sight of your vision and goal of what you want or your Faith and purpose to get what you want.

Let me give you another word of caution here in regard to motives. Beware of the insidious temptation to seek power over others.

Nothing is so pleasant to the unformed or partially developed mind as daydreaming about the exercise of power or dominion over others. The desire to rule for selfish gratification has been the curse of the world to countless human beings for numerous ages.

Today, the main motive in the business and industrial world is the same. Commercial kings, like political kings, are inspired by the lust for power.

Never fall for the temptation to seek authority, to become a controller, to be considered as one who is above the common herd, to impress others by lavish display, and so on.

The mind that seeks mastery over others is the competitive mind, and the competitive mind is not the creative one. It will surely never bring you *lasting* success. In order to conquer your environment and your destiny, it is not at all necessary that you should rule over and take advantage of your fellow brothers and sisters, and indeed, when you fall into the world's struggle for high places, you begin to be conquered by fate and environment, and your success becomes a matter of randomness, chance, and speculation, as you have wrongfully built upon loose footing.

Chapter 15:
You as an "Advancing Person"

"I dream my painting and then I paint my dream."
—Vincent Van Gogh

"What you think you become.
What you feel, you attract.
What you imagine, you create."
—Buddha

"There is a Universal Power, Spirit, and Energy flowing down into and through you that empowers you and never fails to present opportunity to the advancing person who is moving in obedience with Universal Law. To think what you want to think is to think TRUTH, inside-out, regardless of appearances, outside-in."
—P. J. DiNuzzo

W hat I have said in my last chapter applies to the professional person and the wage earner as well as to the man or woman who is engaged in business.

No matter whether you are a physician, a teacher, or a leader, if you can give *increase of life* to others and make them aware of your energy of increase, they will be attracted to you, and you will succeed. The physician who holds the vision of themself as a great and successful healer, and who works toward the complete realization of that vision with emotion, Faith and purpose, as described in my former chapters, will come into such close touch with the Source of Life that they will be phenomenally successful and patients will come to them in throngs.

No one has a greater opportunity to carry into effect the teachings of my book than the practitioner of medicine. It does not matter to which of the various schools they may belong, for the principle of healing is common to all of them and may be reached by all alike. The advancing person in medicine, who holds to a clear mental image of themself as successful, and who obeys my principles of BELIEF, FAITH, PURPOSE, THOUGHT, IMAGINATION, WANT, VISION, GOAL, BURNING-DESIRE, VISUALIZATION, EMOTION, ACTION, ACCEPTANCE, BUOYANCY, and GRATITUDE will cure every curable case they undertake, no matter what remedies they may use.

In the field of leadership, the world cries out for the leader who can teach their followers the true Universal Science of abundant life. Those who master the details of the science of success and Manifesting, together with the allied sciences of being well, of being great, and of winning love, and who teach these details from a position of leadership, will never lack for appreciative followers.

This is the gospel that the world needs, for it will give *increase of life*. Men and women will hear it gladly, and it will give overwhelming support to the leader who brings it to them.

What is now needed is a demonstration of Universal Intelligence's Science of Life from the pulpit of leadership. We want leaders who can not only tell us how but who, in their own persons, will show us how. We need the leader who will themself be successful, healthy, great, and beloved, to teach us how to achieve these things, and when this leader arrives, they will find a numerous and loyal following of the masses.

I AM, I AM, I AM, I AM.

The same is true of the teacher who can inspire children with the Faith and purpose of the Advancing Life. They will never be "out of a job." And any teacher who has this Faith and Purpose can give it to their pupils. They cannot help giving it to them if it is part of their own life and practice.

What is true of the teacher, leader, and physician is true of the lawyer, dentist, plumber, electrician, carpenter, real estate person, insurance agent—of everybody.

The combined mental and personal action I have described is *infallible*, for it cannot fail. Every man and woman who follows my instructions steadily, perseveringly, and to the letter will succeed and *Manifest Anything You Can Imagine*. The Law of the Increase of Life is as mathematically certain in its operation as the Law of Gravity.

Manifesting and success according to Universal Intelligence and Universal Laws is an exact science.

The wage earner will find this as true of their case as of any of the others mentioned. Do not feel that you have no chance to succeed because you are working where there is no visible opportunity for advancement, where wages are small and the cost of living high. Form your clear mental vision and goal of what you want, and begin to act with Faith, emotion, and purpose.

Do all the work you can do, every day, and do each piece of work in a successful manner. Put discipline, effort, and your purpose, into everything you do to Manifest.

To secure advancement, something more is necessary than to be too large for your place.

The person who is certain to advance is the one who is too big for their place, *and* who has a clear concept of what they want to be, *and* who knows that they can become what they want to be, *and* who is determined to be what they want to be.

Fill your present place with the idea of advancing yourself. Hold the Faith and purpose of increase during work hours, after work hours, and before work hours. Hold it in such a way that *every person* who comes in contact with you, whether supervisor, fellow worker, or social acquaintance, will feel the power of purpose vibrations radiating from you so that everyone will get the sense of advancement and increase from you. Men and women will be attracted to you, and if there is no possibility for advancement in your present job, you will very soon see an opportunity to take another job.

There is a Universal Power, Spirit, and energy flowing down into and through you *that empowers you and never fails* to present opportunity to the advancing person who is moving in obedience with Universal Law.

Universal Intelligence cannot help helping you if you act in the Universal Way; Universal Intelligence must do so in order to help Itself and the entire Advancing Universe.

There is nothing in your circumstances, or your social or economic situation, that can keep you down. If you cannot succeed working for a big organization, you can easily succeed elsewhere. And if you begin to move in the Universal Way, you will certainly escape from the "clutches" of big business and get on to your next available, better-fit golden opportunity.

Begin this way of thinking and acting, and your Faith and purpose will make you quick to see any opportunity to better your condition.

Such opportunities will speedily come, for Universal Intelligence, working in all, *and working for you*, will bring them before you.

Do not wait for an opportunity to be all that you want to be. When an opportunity to be more than you are now is presented and you feel impelled toward it, take it. It will be the first step toward a greater opportunity.

There is no such thing possible in this Universe as a lack of opportunities for the person who is living the advancing life.

It is inherent in the *constitution of the cosmos* that all things shall be for you and work together for your good, and you must certainly succeed if you act and think in the Universal Way. So let wage-earning men and women study my book with great care, and enter with confidence into the course of action it prescribes.

It cannot and will not fail.

Chapter 16:

Concluding Observations

"Start today. You have nothing to lose.
But you have your whole life to win."
— Earl Nightingale

"Imagination is everything.
It is the preview of life's coming attractions."
—Albert Einstein

"You will find that every difficulty, problem, and challenge carry
within them the solution for their overcoming and a greater
opportunity for significant advancement going forward."
—P. J. DiNuzzo

any people may scoff at the idea that there is a Universal Intelligence Exact Science of Manifesting, succeeding, and enjoying your Best-Life, instead holding the impression that the supply of wealth is limited, that there is scarcity, and they will insist that social and governmental institutions must be changed before even any considerable number of people can be successful. If they are not willing to Believe, change, improve, grow, and embrace their Best-Life, my book is *not* for them.

Because their Belief and Faith are not true.

If you have an advancing mind, the Faith that you can succeed and move forward and grow with the fixed purpose to succeed, nothing can possibly keep you in poverty.

The more men and women who succeed on the competitive plane, the worse for others. The more who succeed on the creative plane, the better for others.

The economic salvation of the masses can only be accomplished by getting a larger number of people to practice the Universal Scientific Method I have set out in my book and succeed. These people will show others the way and inspire them with a desire for real life, with the Faith that it can be attained, and with the purpose to attain it.

For the present, however, it is enough to know that neither the government under which you live nor your current economic or competitive system of industry and commerce can keep you from succeeding. When you enter into the creative plane of thought, you will rise above all these things and truly become a citizen of another Kingdom.

Always remain neutral, neutral to government, neutral to religion, neutral to politics, and neutral to others who are negative or argumentative.

In order to Manifest and live in harmony with Universal Intelligence at a high-vibration, you must do everything in your power to avoid negativity and low-vibration people and situations at all costs.

Remember again, that your *thought* must be held upon the creative plane, and you are never for an instant to be betrayed into having a scarcity mindset and regarding the supply as limited, or into acting on the conflict-filled level of competition.

Whenever you do fall into your old ways of thought, correct yourself instantly, for when you are in the competitive mind, you have lost the cooperation, vibration, and frequency of the mind of Universal Intelligence.

Do not spend any time on planning how you will meet possible emergencies in the future, except to the extent the necessary policies may literally affect your actions *today*. You are to be focused on and concerned with doing today's work in a successful manner, and not with emergencies that may or may not arise tomorrow. You can attend to them as they present themselves.

Do not concern yourself with questions as to how you shall surmount obstacles that may loom upon your business or financial horizon unless you can see plainly and absolutely that your course must be altered *today* in order to avoid them.

No matter how tremendous an obstruction may appear at a distance, you will find that if you go on in the Universal Way, it will disappear as you approach it, or that a way over, through, or around it will appear.

Know this in your heart of hearts.

No possible combination of circumstances can defeat a man or woman who is proceeding to succeed along Universal Intelligence Scientific Lines. No man or woman who obeys Universal Law can fail to Manifest and succeed, any more than one can multiply two by two and fail to get four.

Give no anxious thought to possible disasters, obstacles, panics, or unfavorable combinations of circumstances. It is time enough to meet such things when they present themselves before you in the present.

You will find that every difficulty, problem, and challenge carry within them the solution for their overcoming and a greater opportunity for significant advancement going forward.

If you come into contact with news or social media that states that a recession or economic slowdown, or any other negative statement for that matter, is heading your way and is "inevitable," your immediate verbal and mental response is always... "I refuse to participate."

"I AM So Happy and Grateful Now That I can and do create my own economy."

"I AM So Happy and Grateful Now That when faced with challenges or problems, I always respond 'that is good,' for I know in my heart of hearts that the true and best solution and a greater opportunity always lie within."

Guard your speech and your "self-talk." Never speak of yourself, your affairs, or of anything else in a negative, discouraged, or discouraging way.

Eliminate *all* negative self-talk, conversations, and people.

Positive self-talk is one of the most powerful forces that Universe Intelligence makes available for you to succeed.

You can truly *speak or call it into existence.*

Control what you can control and your dreams and wishes will be satisfied beyond your wildest current imagination.

Never steal defeat from the jaws of victory, which is easily within your reach, by using negative self-talk.

Never admit the possibility of failure, or speak in a way that even infers any chance of failure.

Never speak of the times as being hard, or of business conditions as being doubtful. Times may be hard and business doubtful for those who are on the competitive plane, but they can *never* be so for you, for you can create what you want, and you are above fear.

You can only be in either a *"fear"* or a *"faith"* mindset. You must chose to Believe in one or the other. With Universal Intelligence at your back and on your side, if you are going to place your Belief in anything, always place it in Faith, Manifesting, and Happiness.

Remember the Universal Law of Attraction... *like attracts like.*

When others are having hard times and poor business, you will find your greatest opportunities.

Train yourself to think of and to look upon the world as something that is *becoming*, that is fully expressing, expanding, increasing, and growing, and train yourself to regard seeming problems, challenges, or evil as being only that which is undeveloped. Always speak in terms of advancement; to do otherwise is to deny your Faith, and to deny your Faith is to lose it.

Never allow yourself to feel disappointed. You may expect to have a certain thing at a certain time and not get it at that time, and this will initially appear to you as a failure.

But if you hold to your Faith, you will find that what you thought was failure really wasn't failure at all.

Go on in the Universal Way, and if you do not receive that thing, you will receive something that's so much better that you will see that the seeming failure was really a great success and that Universal Intelligence, in Its grand wisdom, actually did you a favor.

There is not and cannot be failure... instead, rest assured that something bigger and/or better is coming your way.

Know in your heart of hearts that if you are living in the Universal Way and you do not receive something, it is only because the Universe has something bigger and/or better on Its way to you.

There once was a student of Universal Science who had set their mind on making a certain business deal that seemed to them at the time to be very desirable, and they worked for some time to bring it about. When the crucial time came, the thing failed in a totally inexplicable way. It was as if some unseen influence had been working secretly against them. They were not disappointed; on the contrary, they thanked Universal Intelligence that their desire had been overruled, and they went steadily on with a *grateful mind*. Within a few weeks, an opportunity came their way that was so much better that they would not have made the first deal on any account, and they saw that a Universal Mind that knew more than they knew had prevented them from losing the greater good by entangling themself with the lesser opportunity.

That is the way every seeming failure will work out for you.

If you keep your BELIEF, FAITH, PURPOSE, THOUGHT, IMAGINATION, WANT, VISION, GOAL, BURNING-DESIRE, VISUALIZATION, EMOTION, ACTION, ACCEPTANCE, BUOY-ANCY, and GRATITUDE, and do, every day, all that can be done that day, doing each separate action in an efficient and successful manner, you are certain under Universal Intelligence to *Manifest Anything* You *Can Imagine*.

When you make what appears to you as a failure, it is often because you have not asked for enough. Keep on, and a larger thing than you are seeking will certainly come to you.

You will not fail because you lack the necessary talent to do what you wish to do. If you go on as I have directed, you will develop all the talent that is necessary for the doing of your work and the Manifestation of your goal.

It is not within the scope of my book to deal with the science of cultivating talent, but it is as certain and simple as the process of succeeding.

However, do not hesitate or waver for fear that when you come to any certain place, you will fail for lack of ability. Keep right on, and when you come to that place, the ability will be furnished to you.

The same source of ability that enabled the untaught Abraham Lincoln to do the greatest work the United States government ever accomplished by a single person is open to you. You may draw upon all the mind there is for wisdom to use in meeting the responsibilities that are laid upon you.

Go on, my fellow brothers and sisters, in confidence with a strong self-image and with full Faith.

Study my book. Study it every day. Study at least one page every day.

Make it your constant companion until you have mastered all the ideas contained within it and Manifested your goals.

While you are getting firmly established in this Faith, you will do well to give up or reduce most recreations, pleasures, alcohol, and drugs, and to stay away from negativity and places where ideas conflicting with Universal Intelligence's ideas are advanced in social media, technology, lectures, presentations, or sermons. Do not read pessimistic or conflicting literature or get into arguments on the matter. Spend most of your leisure time contemplating your vision and your goal with emotion at the level like that of a child on Christmas morning, cultivating Gratitude, and reading my book. It contains all you need to know of Universal Intelligence's Science to *Manifest Anything You Can Imagine*, and you will find that I have all the essentials summed up in my following chapter.

Chapter 17:

Summary of My Universal Intelligence Science of Success, Happiness, and Manifesting Your Goal

"If you want your children to be intelligent, read them fairy tales. If you want them to be very intelligent, read them more fairy tales."
—Albert Einstein

"The only thing that can grow is the thing you give energy to."
—Ralph Waldo Emerson

"My Subconscious Mind, in a very soft unspoken tone and message, provides me with the answer and gives me one or maybe two seconds to recognize it and act on it. The longer you wait, the worse it is for your decision-making success as your 'paradigm' starts to take over and typically provides a hundred reasons why you should not take action."
—P. J. DiNuzzo

S pend most of your leisure time contemplating your vision and your goal with emotion at the level like that of a child on Christmas morning.

This Universe was created eons and eons ago.

All creation is complete.

Your perfect and infinite "thought universe" was created to remain forever in harmony and was instilled, embedded, and "programmed" for you and all for continuous and infinite expression, expansion, increase, growth, success, and happiness.

The "thought universe" you live in was filled for your enjoyment by Universal Intelligence with *infinite wisdom, love, life, abundance, joy, and harmony.*

Your Spiritual Spark, Spiritual DNA, and Spirit are perfect.

You have been given every tool you need to Manifest, succeed, and live your Best-Life.

You have been given every tool you need to *Manifest Anything You Can Imagine.*

You live on earth... in a "thought world" within a "thought universe."

You have been chosen and blessed even insofar as reading my book as you have directly received an invitation and an offer to be educated by Universal Intelligence.

Be appreciative and Grateful... Very few people even make it this far.

Be continuously Grateful that not only does Universal Intelligence know your name, but it also truly loves you and emotionally desires for you to co-create with It and live your Best-Life, every single day!

Final Summary

"In order to Manifest and live in harmony with Universal Intelligence at a high-vibration, you must do everything in your power to avoid negativity and low-vibration people and situations at all costs. If your thoughts are negative, you will attract more negative. If your thoughts are positive, you will attract more positive."
—P. J. DiNuzzo

There is a Universal Original Intelligent Formless Thinking Substance from which all things are made, and which, in Its original state, permeates, penetrates, and fills the interspaces of the entire Infinite Universe.

Your thought in this Thinking Substance produces the thought-form and thing that you visualize in your thought.

You can form things in your thought, and by impressing your thought-form upon Universal Intelligent Substance, you can cause the thing you think about to be created in Universal Intelligence's Quantum Field.

In order to do this, you must pass from the competitive to the creative mind, otherwise you cannot be in harmony with the Universal Subconscious Mind, which is always creative and never competitive in Spirit.

You come into full harmony with the Universal Intelligent Substance by entertaining a lively and sincere Gratitude for the blessings It bestows upon you. For it is Gratitude filled with emotion that unifies your mind with the Intelligence of Substance so that your thoughts are received by the Formless. You can remain upon the creative plane only by uniting yourself with the Formless Intelligence through a burning-desire along with a deep and continuous feeling of emotion and Gratitude.

You should form a clear and definite mental image of the goal and thing you wish to have, do, or become, and you should hold this mental image in your thoughts and in your mind, while being deeply Grateful to Universal Intelligence that all your desires are granted unto you.

In your wishes to succeed, you should spend your leisure hours in contemplation of your vision and your goal, and in earnest appreciation that the reality is being given to you.

Too much stress cannot be laid on the importance of your imagination and frequent visualization of your goal and mental image, coupled with your unwavering burning-desire, emotion, high-vibration, buoyancy, Faith, and continuous Gratitude.

For this is the process through which your thought-form impression is given to the Formless Substance and Universal Intelligence's creative forces are set in motion.

Universal Intelligence's Creative Energy works through the established channels of natural growth and of the existing economic, industrial, and social order.

All that is included in your mental image will surely be brought to you as you follow the instructions I have given above, *and* as your Faith does not waver.

What you want will come to you through the ways of established trade, industry, and commerce.

In order to receive your own when it shall come to you, you must be active in performing *efficient action*, and this activity can only consist of more than filling your present place.

You must keep in mind your purpose of Manifesting your goal through the realization of your mental image.

And you must do, every day, all that can be done that day, taking care to do each action in a successful manner.

You must give to every man and woman with whom you interact a Use Value in excess of the Cash Value you receive from them, so much so that each transaction makes for more life, and you must hold the advancing thought in your mind so that the impression of increase will be communicated to all with whom you come into contact.

As you practice my foregoing instructions, you will certainly succeed and Manifest Anything You Can Imagine, and the success you achieve will be in exact proportion to the definiteness of your VISION, GOAL, IMAGINATION, WANT, and THOUGHT, the fixity of your PURPOSE, the steadiness of your BELIEF, FAITH, BURNING-DESIRE, VISUALIZATION, ACTION, BUOYANCY, and ACCEPTANCE, along with the depth of your EMOTION and GRATITUDE.

"The Secret"

"Weak people revenge. Strong people forgive.
Intelligent people ignore."
—Albert Einstein

"The 'secret' is that you Manifest and create with your thought-forms
combined with your body of emotions. It is mind over matter, for
your mind and thoughts combined with your emotions rule all."
—P. J. DiNuzzo

Universal Intelligence has launched the dawning of a new age of prosperity, abundance, wealth, peace, and tranquility, and through your and other's Spiritual Being, you and all may attain these goals.

You live in a thought-forming world within a perfect and Infinite Thought-Forming Universe.

The ancients and masters of our world knew this.

Universal Intelligence created this world to harness the creative thought-form.

Universal Intelligence is not the lesser but rather the more of humankind.

Universal Intelligence wants you to flow, move forward, and advance.

You can own, possess, and enjoy all of that which you desire.

You have a brilliant sun of opportunities before you.

This world and you are not meant for poverty.

Never lose Faith, for there is more to life for you than poverty... much, much more.

You are a Beloved Child of Universal Intelligence regardless of age, race, creed, religion, gender, or ethnicity.

You, along with every man, woman, and child deserve the right of free will, abundance, wealth, food, prosperity, clothing, shelter, happiness, and to rise above poverty.

Universal Intelligence desires freedom and truth for you and for you to be free along with all men, women, and children, regardless of age, race, creed, religion, gender, or ethnicity.

You, along with every life of humanity, deserve the wealth of abundance.

Spirit brings forth abundance, and for you it is always attainable.

Universal Intelligence and you are the *masterminds* of your Spirit, your heart, your mind, your body, and your thought.

You are a *thought being* at one with the Infinite Universal Power of your mind.

Your thoughts when combined with your heart are a Universal Creative Force.

You create your world yourself through your own thoughts and through your own emotions.

Positive thoughts will deliver unto you positive results, while negative thoughts will deliver unto you negative results.

If you fear that which will come to you, it will come to you.

If you worry, you will attract more worry, and if you fear debt, you will attract more debt.

If you release all of your negative thoughts and release all of your fear, then only that which is positive will come to you and replace it.

Obstacles, challenges, and problems may appear before you, but never forget that they are but Universal Intelligence's teaching tools.

They are there for you to persevere, Manifest, succeed, increase, expand, and grow.

Fear is the defeat of your *mastermind* and your alignment with the Universal Way. Have Faith and Gratitude, let go of all that you have known, and open up to the world of possibilities that Universal Intelligence has made ready especially for you.

It is the Universal Way and process of your thoughts in combination with your emotions and desires that create abundance or a lack thereof.

Each and every step of Manifesting your dreams and wishes is attainable. It is as if you are stretching for something on a shelf that is within your reach.

To Manifest the goal of your dreams and wishes, you should always strive to the worthwhile practice of maintaining a sense of buoyancy, high-vibration, happiness, and Gratitude, and strive to live in the comfort of knowing in your mind and in your heart of hearts that all you desire is here waiting for you.

To Manifest, you must join with your Inner Child and forget what you have been taught and become one with your Inner Child of imagination.

To Manifest, you are to maintain your positive thinking along with your emotional want and burning-desire, and you shall surely achieve your goal.

"The secret" is that you Manifest and create with your thought-forms combined with your body of emotions. It is mind over matter, for your mind and thoughts combined with your emotions rule all.

Your Spirit is Perfect.

Through these applied principles, Universal Intelligence shall bring forth growth and abundance to you and all of humanity, ushering in a "New Thought" age of abundance and riches, along with the lessening of poverty.

Know all this... and you will surely be on your most golden path of happiness and co-creating your Best-Life in harmony with Universal Intelligence as you <u>*Manifest Anything*</u> *You Can Imagine.*

You and I have the Perfect Spiritual Spark, Perfect Spiritual DNA, and Perfect Spirit of Universal Intelligence within us; therefore...

I AM, I AM, I AM, I AM.

Final Thoughts

"Thoughts Create things. Thoughts Make things. Thoughts Become things. Thoughts are on Frequencies, and they are all interconnected. Thoughts travel faster than the speed of light. Thoughts travel through any and all mass. Every single thought of yours creates a thought-form. Thinking Substance takes the form of Its Thought and moves according to the thought. You attract and become what you Think about most often. The Law of Attraction Manifests the thing that you think about, both positive and negative."
—P. J. DiNuzzo

My final thoughts are a reiteration of Supreme Power's Core Message that is being delivered throughout my book and through me directly to you and those you love.

The Universal Truths that I AM sharing directly from Universal Intelligence are first and foremost for the most in need among us.

Those who need true and real hope the most.

It is for my fellow brothers and sisters from all walks of life, women and children, every creed, every race.

With heartfelt love, it is most especially for the downtrodden, across our entire world, to uplift themselves and rise out of poverty and despair.

Universal Intelligence's intentions are for no poverty in this world, in your life, or for any restrictions on your happiness.

We and we alone place restrictions on ourselves and our lives.

Universal Intelligence never has and never will.

If you allow the outside world in to control your life, it becomes destructive, and it erodes your Universal Intelligence and Supreme Power Given Rights of Creation that lie directly within your hands.

By living with Belief and Faith, *inside-out*, as Universal Intelligence intends, you and you alone are meant and designed to be the only controller of your destiny and Manifestations.

Your want, grown into a desire, and then filled with emotion, creates a burning-desire, and this burning-desire then creates a "gravitational pull" toward you from Universal Intelligence beyond your wildest imagination.

I include *all* in my book, and I AM imploring *you* to open yourself up to Universal Intelligence and Its Truths and let It touch your heart and inspire you to take action to <u>Manifest Anything</u> You Can Imagine.

No matter who you are or where you are in your life right now, you can enjoy living in the happiness of your dreams and wishes as Universal Intelligence truly intends...

ALL HAS BEEN DELIVERED THROUGH ME AND I HAVE SHARED THE ENTIRETY OF IT WITH YOU AND I DEDICATE THE REST OF MY LIFE TO HELPING YOU TO <u>Manifest Anything</u> *You Can Imagine.*

Afterword by Nick Pavlidis

I f you've read this far, you have in your possession a secret that can help you achieve your wildest dreams.

You know the mindset that has helped some of the most successful people in the world achieve levels of health, wealth, and happiness far beyond what most people ever dream possible.

And, better yet, you know a secret that anyone can use no matter where they live or how much money they make.

But that's not all. You've also been introduced to a coach and mentor in P. J. DiNuzzo who wants you to succeed and has put in place several ways for you to start applying the principles you have just learned.

You've met a coach and mentor in P. J. DiNuzzo who wants more for you than he wants for himself, who truly desires in his heart of hearts to help you achieve your dreams.

I've personally helped thousands of people plan, produce, and publish their books via group learning and individual one-on-one support.

I've learned during that time that every author's journey to writing a book is unique. Many people want to write a book to grow their business, become a thought leader, or tell a story they want the world to hear. Some want to supplement or replace their income through books and other products and services. There's nothing wrong with any of those motives. The world needs those books. It needs for people to share inspiring stories or messages. It needs authors to be able to support themselves financially. It needs people to want to write books.

Very rarely, however, does somebody come to me and say they "have" to write their book. Very rarely does somebody tell me they have no choice but to write their book.

Very few write because they feel they truly must, that they have a message they were born to share, almost as if they were directed by a higher power to share an important message.

Very few come to the pages with a mission that's bigger than themselves.

But that's exactly what P. J. DiNuzzo told me about the book you just read.

This book, he told me, wasn't the book he wanted to write. He had written three other books—important books to help people invest money, build wealth, and achieve other important personal, family, and philanthropic goals, and minimize their tax burdens. And he loved those books. He wrote them because he wanted to share some of the most tactical information and direction with the world.

But this book was "different," he said when he first shared his vision for the book with me.

I've known P. J. for several years. I have worked closely with him during that time, speaking with him at least weekly for the first couple of years and practically daily ever since.

I even consulted with him on his second and third books and helped him reach enough readers to hit multiple bestseller lists, including the *Wall Street Journal* and *USA Today*, as well as hitting the #1 spot on Amazon's nonfiction bestseller list and the #1 overall book on BarnesandNoble.com.

In other words, his first three books have helped a lot of people.

More importantly, I've seen what P. J.'s like when nobody else is watching. I've talked with him when nobody is expecting him to talk about investing, supporting wealthy growth-minded families, or saving money on taxes.

When P. J. told me about this book, I immediately knew it would be special. I could tell that this book was one that he felt he *had* to write. What's more, although many authors think of ideas bigger than themselves and some even invest a lot of time and money spreading the word, very few invest the time, money, and emotional resources necessary to bring a message to the masses without expecting anything in return. Very few people move forward without a clear return on investment in sight.

But that's exactly what P. J. asked me: how to get this message in front of as many people as possible irrespective of their ability to send him a single penny.

"You could definitely write a book about it," I advised. "That would allow people to access the information for as little as many people spend on weekly coffee runs. And those who couldn't could possibly borrow it from their local library."

He wanted more. What about the people whose libraries didn't have copies and didn't have enough money to even buy the book?

So we set up ManifestAnythingFree.com for anyone to get or even gift a copy of this book to someone else.

What about people who wanted to go deeper with the subject matter? P. J. invested tremendous time and resources building out PJMindset-CoachInstitute.com, an online platform with videos and other resources for people to do exactly that. And if someone can't pay, they don't have to.

Moreover, his publisher is engaging in efforts to bring the book to interested publishing companies internationally to help even more people. And P. J. has already personally invested in getting the process started by hiring a Spanish-language translator to create Spanish versions of this book and the content on PJMindsetCoachInstitute.com.

Some come with an idea that's bigger than them. But very few invest the time, money, and emotional resources necessary to bring a message to as many people.

And even fewer do so without concern for an "ROI."

But P. J. DiNuzzo did.

Not because he wanted to, although he did want to.

Because he "had" to.

This is his purpose... his calling... his legacy.

To help *you* build your dream life and manifest everything and *anything* your heart desires.

Accept his offer of help. And if you can't pay him a penny, that's okay.

All you need to do is take action.

—Nick Pavlidis

Appendix I:
Your Daily Affirmation—
First Half

"I believe you can speak things into existence."
—Jay-Z

"If you keep your BELIEF, FAITH, PURPOSE, THOUGHT, IMAGINATION, WANT, VISION, GOAL, BURNING-DESIRE, VISUALIZATION, EMOTION, ACTION, ACCEPTANCE, BUOYANCY, and GRATITUDE, and do, every day, all that can be done that day, doing each separate action in an efficient and successful manner, you are certain under Universal Intelligence to <u>Manifest Anything</u> You Can Imagine."
—P. J. DiNuzzo

I AM So Happy and Grateful Now That...
I AM So Happy and Grateful Now That I treat every person I meet as though they are the most important person on earth... starting with myself... every single morning.

I AM So Happy and Grateful Now That I want the same for my fellow brothers and sisters as I want for myself.

I AM So Happy and Grateful Now That I *never* sit in judgment of any other person.

I AM So Happy and Grateful Now That I forgive with love anyone who has ever harmed me or even intended to harm me, and I release them, and myself, from my thoughts.

I AM So Happy and Grateful Now That My Spiritual Spark, My Spirit, and My Spiritual DNA are perfect in every way and are truly the real me, and I know that I AM an Eternal Spiritual Being having a limited physical experience.

I AM So Happy and Grateful Now That I was made in Universal Intelligence's likeness, and I know that Universal Intelligence and the Universal Subconscious Mind live within me and that I AM constantly connected with It, to It, and to All.

I AM So Happy and Grateful Now That Universal Intelligence has created a perfect and Infinite Universe for the expression, expansion, increase, growth, and happiness of me, others, and Itself.

I AM So Happy and Grateful Now That Universal Intelligence knows my name and loves me enough to extend an invitation to me to teach me Its Universal Ways so that I may succeed, grow, and be happy to my heart's desire.

I AM So Happy and Grateful Now That I live in a "thought world" within a perfect and infinite "thought universe."

I AM So Happy and Grateful Now That Universal Intelligence loves me and desires for me to co-create with It and live my Best-Life every single day.

I AM So Happy and Grateful Now That I live in Universal Intelligence's perfect and infinite sea of wisdom, love, life, abundance, joy, and harmony.

I AM So Happy and Grateful Now That I know I AM living my life's purpose, enjoy how I AM growing, and am aligned in harmony with the Universe.

I AM So Happy and Grateful Now That I recognize that "suggestion" and "auto-suggestion" (suggestions from myself to myself) into my Subconscious Mind are the most powerful forces on earth available to me to Manifest and live my Best-Life.

I AM So Happy and Grateful Now That I have a "magic lamp" in my Subconscious Mind that gives me and acts on *unlimited* wishes and suggestions (good or bad) that I deliver to It or allow It to hear.

I AM So Happy and Grateful Now That I understand how special my "higher-faculties" are and that they (WIP RIM—will, imagination, perception, reason, intuition, and memory) are my Universal Way tools for success and to Manifest my goal.

I AM So Happy and Grateful Now That I live every day in a mindset of abundance, not scarcity.

I AM So Happy and Grateful Now That I live every day in a creative, not competitive, mindset

I AM So Happy and Grateful Now That I live every day in a mindset of Faith, not fear.

I AM So Happy and Grateful Now That I live every day in a mindset of high-vibration and buoyancy, not low-vibration.

I AM So Happy and Grateful Now That I understand that my goals, which comprise the whole of my vision, are primarily for growth, not achievement.

I AM So Happy and Grateful Now That I have continuous Belief and Faith in Manifesting my goal, and I *never* ask if, how, or when.

I AM So Happy and Grateful Now That I AM a co-creator with Universal Intelligence.

I AM So Happy and Grateful Now That I AM, I AM, I AM, I AM... I AM, I AM, I AM, I AM.

Appendix II:
Your Daily Affirmation— Second Half

*"To believe in the things you see and touch is no belief at all,
but to believe in the unseen is a triumph and a blessing."*
—Abraham Lincoln

*"You can only be in either a 'fear' or a 'faith' mindset. You must
choose to Believe in one or the other. With Universal Intelligence at
your back and on your side, if you are going to place your Belief in
anything, always place it in Faith, Manifesting, and happiness."*
—P. J. DiNuzzo

I AM So Happy and Grateful Now That...

I AM So Happy and Grateful Now That there is a Universal Original Intelligent Formless Thinking Substance, which operates under Universal Laws, from which all things are made, and which, in its original state, permeates, penetrates, and fills the interspaces of the entire Infinite Universe.

I AM So Happy and Grateful Now That as I Manifest my goal my thought in this Universal Thinking Substance produces the thought-form and thing that I visualize in my thought.

I AM So Happy and Grateful Now That my thoughts produce, make, and create things.

I AM So Happy and Grateful Now That I can form things in my thought, and by impressing my thought-form upon Universal Intelligent Substance, I can co-create and Manifest the thing and goal I think about with Universal Intelligence in Its Quantum Field to be physically delivered to me through my efficient actions.

I AM So Happy and Grateful Now That I always pass from the competitive to the creative mind, otherwise I could not be in harmony as I AM with the Universal Subconscious Mind, which is always creative and never competitive in Spirit.

I AM So Happy and Grateful Now That I AM in full harmony with Universal Intelligent Substance because of entertaining a lively and sincere Gratitude for the blessings it bestows upon me. For it is my Gratitude that unifies my mind with the Intelligence of Substance so that my thoughts are received by the Formless. I remain upon the creative plane by uniting myself with the Formless Intelligence through a burning-desire along with my deep and continuous feeling of emotion and Gratitude.

I AM So Happy and Grateful Now That I form a clear and definite thought-form and mental image of the goal and thing I wish to have, do, or become, and I hold this mental image in my thoughts and in my mind, all while being deeply Grateful to Universal Intelligence as my desires and goals are Manifested and granted unto me over and over again.

I AM So Happy and Grateful Now That in my burning-desire and wishes to succeed and Manifest, I spend my leisure hours contemplating my vision and my goal, and remain in earnest appreciation and Gratitude as the reality is being given to me.

I AM So Happy and Grateful Now That I focus on the importance of my imagination and frequent visualization of my goal and mental image, coupled with my unwavering burning-desire, emotion, high-vibration, buoyancy, Belief, Faith, and continuous Gratitude.

I AM So Happy and Grateful Now That I know in my heart of hearts that this is the process through which I co-create and my thought-form impression is given to the Formless Substance, and Universal Intelligence's Creative Forces are set in motion for my benefit.

I AM So Happy and Grateful Now That I Believe that Universal Intelligence's Creative Energy works through the established channels of natural growth, and of the existing economic, industrial, and social order.

I AM So Happy and Grateful Now That All that I include in my mental image is brought to me, over and over again, as I follow my instructions, *and* as my Faith does not waver.

I AM So Happy and Grateful Now That What I want comes to me through the ways of established trade, industry, and commerce.

I AM So Happy and Grateful Now That as I receive my own as it comes to me, I am always performing efficient action and my activity always consists of me more than filling my present place.

I AM So Happy and Grateful Now That I constantly hold in my mind the purpose of Manifesting my goal through the realization of my mental image.

I AM So Happy and Grateful Now That I do, every day, all that I can and should do each day, taking care to do each action in a successful manner.

I AM So Happy and Grateful Now That I give to every man and woman with whom I interact a Use Value in excess of the Cash Value I receive from them, so much so that each transaction makes for more life, and I hold the advancing thought in my mind so that my impression of increase is communicated to all with whom I come into contact.

I AM So Happy and Grateful Now That as I practice my foregoing instructions and ritual, I continuously succeed and *Manifest Anything*

I Can Imagine, and the success I achieve is in exact proportion to the definiteness of my VISION, GOAL, IMAGINATION, WANT, and THOUGHT, the fixity of my PURPOSE, the steadiness of my BELIEF, FAITH, BURNING-DESIRE, VISUALIZATION, ACTION, BUOY-ANCY, and ACCEPTANCE, along with the depth of my EMOTION and GRATITUDE.

Glossary and Concepts to Live By

"You and I get to protect our Subconscious Minds, which I refer to as your 'Magic Lamp,' and 'P. J.'s Magic Lamp' when I talk about my Subconscious Mind. And we reject or cancel any and all 'negative suggestions' from ourselves, others, or outside sources, into our Subconscious Minds at all costs."
—P. J DiNuzzo

1 Percent Better: Your *daily ritual* includes your goal of getting *1 percent better* every single day. Getting 1 percent better is a goal you *know* is doable and that you can achieve every day. Develop a *winning streak* of getting 1 percent better every single day, and it will propel you to achieve your Quantum Leap.

10,000 Hours: Typically, in order to enjoy success in any new career, job, business, or endeavor, it requires about 10,000 hours or approximately five years to acquire a critical mass of the new skill set and knowledge. You can certainly *Manifest Anything You Can Imagine* sooner, but a lot of life is about understanding and managing expectations.

Abundance: Your mind can only live in either a mindset of abundance or a mindset of scarcity. In order for you to *Manifest Anything You Can Imagine*, you must be in a mindset of abundance. It includes all forms of wealth and prosperity, including material wealth, health, happiness, and relationships that are achieved through the Universal Way. Abundance is all forms of wealth and prosperity, while scarcity is the Belief in a lack of resources or opportunities, which leads to negative outcomes.

Acceptance: One of P. J.'s Manifest Recipe's Fifteen (15) Key Ingredients to *Manifest Anything* You Can Imagine. Acceptance is one of the final actions and hurdles you will need to succeed at in order to Manifest your goal. You will face it right before the moment or time that you are to receive your goal. There are a surprising number of times when people do everything correctly in harmony with co-creating with Universal Intelligence but end up *blowing* it at the end of the process. You must not doubt yourself or question whether you are worthy. Your paradigm will make one last ditch effort to sabotage you and your Manifested goal right at the end before you physically receive it.

Action: One of P. J.'s Manifest Recipe's Fifteen (15) Key Ingredients to *Manifest Anything* You Can Imagine. Action is one of the key elements in your process of Manifesting what you desire. Your actions, specifically your efficient actions, enable you to *grab* your goal as it is moving toward you from your thoughts that initiated your goal. Your thoughts initially form your goal with a thought-form, and your actions allow you to complete the *physical-back* of your Manifested goal so you can accept it, grab it, and enjoy it.

Advancing Person: As you learn and succeed at your efficient action and in delivering your impression of increase to your fellow brothers and sisters, people will begin to view you as an advancing person often without you even saying a word. As an advancing person, you enjoy for yourself as well as help others succeed with expression, expansion, increase, growth, and happiness.

Affirmation: Always start with "I AM So Happy and Grateful Now That..." Affirmations are most powerful when used in a daily ritual. Combining emotion, buoyancy, Gratitude, and auto-suggestion with discipline on a daily basis is a key element in your success of Manifesting your goal, dreams, and wishes. An Affirmation is a positive statement that aligns your thoughts and Beliefs with your desired outcomes, and it helps you to Manifest them into reality through the power of your intention. Affirmations are a positive declaration or statement spoken in the first person and in the present tense that describes in exact terms what you want to accomplish, what you want to do, who you want to be, what you want to have, and how you want to live your life. It is a positive declaration about yourself in the first person (I), spoken in the present tense (I AM), and specifically describes your desire.

Attitude: Produced by the power, Spirit, and energy flowing down into your Conscious Mind, which creates the feelings in your Subconscious Mind, which in turn cause your body to take action and produce results. Your mind is either in a positive attitude or a negative attitude. You can look at the same exact information, experience, or interaction, and come away with and justify either a positive attitude or a negative attitude. How are you going to live your life? It is all up to you to decide which mindset you want to be in and live in.

Auto-Suggestion: A suggestion from yourself to yourself. The last auto-suggestion that you give and place into your Subconscious Mind right before you fall asleep is extraordinarily important and powerful. Suggestions are the most powerful force on earth and in the Universe. It is the *mustard seed* starting point from which every goal you achieve originates and grows. You have a *magic lamp* inside of you within your Subconscious Mind that takes immediate action on any suggestion that you or any other person, entity, or format make into it. Your Subconscious Mind is trusting you to protect it and assumes that any suggestion given to it from someone or something else meets with your approval and that you want to Manifest it.

Awareness: Neville Goddard is one of the all-time experts regarding awareness. Awareness is the fantastic and limitless world that resides within you and your understanding of what this world enables you to Manifest in order to achieve any dream or wish that you can think of within the rules of nature.

Belief: One of P. J.'s Manifest Recipe's Fifteen (15) Key Ingredients to *Manifest Anything You Can Imagine*. Belief is one of your two initial building blocks along with Faith. You must Believe that (1) Universal Intelligence and the Universal Subconscious Mind created a Perfect and Infinite Universe for you and your fellow brothers and sisters, (2) you live in a Thought World within a Thought Universe, (3) the Universe is ruled by Universal Laws, (4) Universal Intelligence has extended an invitation to you and wants to teach you how to Manifest and succeed, and (5) Universal Intelligence knows your name, loves you, and desires for you to co-create with It and truly wants you to live your Best-Life.

Best-Life: Universal Intelligence, the Universal Subconscious Mind, and the Universal Laws have your Best-Life ready and waiting for you. You just need to embrace It. You can *Manifest Anything You Can Imagine* and enjoy your Best-Life of health, wealth, happiness, companionship, or any other goal, dream, or wish you desire. My entire book is dedicated to you and teaching, leading, and guiding you to co-create with Universal Intelligence and enjoy your Best-Life.

Body: Your body is one of the three major elements, along with your Conscious Mind and your Subconscious Mind, that make up what I refer to as your mind. When most people are asked what their mind is, they respond that their mind is their *brain*. Your brain is no more your mind than your nose or toes are. Your body is an *instrument* of your mind.

Buoyancy: One of P. J.'s Manifest Recipe's Fifteen (15) Key Ingredients to *Manifest Anything You Can Imagine*. Buoyancy is synonymous with you being in a state of *high-vibration*. Your goal is to remain in a state of Buoyancy at all times. Think of yourself as a fisherman's *bobber* in a pond. No matter how far you pull the bobber down under the water, it pops right back up to the surface above the water every time. Buoyancy refers to you continually maintaining a positive and optimistic attitude in the face of challenges, which is important for Manifesting your desired outcomes and overcoming obstacles.

Burning-Desire: One of P. J.'s Manifest Recipe's Fifteen (15) Key Ingredients to *Manifest Anything You Can Imagine*. After you have decided what you truly *want*, your want lives in your Conscious Mind. If you want it bad enough, you can push it down into and deposit it in the *treasury* of your Subconscious Mind and turn it into a *desire*. Your objective is to maintain your desire, with emotion, as a burning-desire. A burning-desire is a deep and intense longing that fuels your actions and propels you toward your goal with unwavering focus and determination. Your continuous burning-desire filled with emotion are the fuel that moves your entire

Manifesting process and allows you to grab and embrace your goal, wish, and dream.

Co-Create: A life-changing power that you possess to create hand in hand with Universal Intelligence, the Universal Subconscious Mind, and the Universal Laws. Your ability to use your higher-faculties WIP RIM (will, imagination, perception, reason, intuition, and memory) in harmony with the Universal Laws empower you to *Manifest Anything You Can Imagine*.

Conscious Mind: Your Conscious Mind is one of the three major elements, along with your Subconscious Mind and your body, that make up what I refer to as your mind. When most people are asked what their mind is, they respond that their mind is their *brain*. Your brain is no more your mind than your nose or toes are. Your Conscious Mind is your *objective mind*, which deals with logic and reason. It is your intellectual thinking mind that accepts, rejects, chooses, and originates. It is connected to and receives input directly from your five senses (sight, smell, taste, hearing, and touch) as well as all outside sources (other people, other things, news, social media, television, ego, etc.). Through your higher-faculty of reason, your Conscious Mind is your primary line of defense for protecting your Subconscious Mind from improper or bad suggestions, which you can do by *canceling* or *rejecting* the negative suggestions immediately. Your Conscious Mind directs your thoughts and identifies your *want*. Your Conscious Mind is very powerful. Think of its energy and power as a computer processing chip the size of your fist vs. your Subconscious Mind, which has the energy and power of a computer processing chip the size of an entire football field... stacked all the way up into and beyond the clouds above you.

Desire: Your desire lives in your subjective and emotion-driven Subconscious Mind. If you want something intensely enough, you can deposit your want into the rich *treasury* of your Subconscious Mind as a desire. You are on the correct road moving in the right direction to *Manifest Anything You Can Imagine* when you convert your desire into a burning-desire continuously filled with emotion.

Divine Operation: As eloquently described by Thomas Troward your mind is a center of divine operation. "My mind is a center of Divine operation. The Divine operation is always for expansion and fuller expression, and this means the production of something beyond what has gone before, something entirely new, not included in the past experience, though proceeding out of it by an orderly sequence of growth. Therefore, since the Divine cannot change its inherent nature, it must operate in the same manner with me; consequently, in my own special world, of which I am the center, it will move forward to produce new conditions, always in advance of any that have gone before."

Double-Binding Message: A double-binding message is a concept from communication theory and psychology that involves contradictory messages that create confusion and anxiety in individuals. It's when you send two or more conflicting messages, affirmations, or actions to your Subconscious Mind. My first question to you if you want someone to love you is, do you love yourself? If you do not love and Believe in yourself, you are sending a double-binding message to the Universe and you will never Manifest successfully.

Efficient Action: In order to *Manifest Anything You Can Imagine*, you must do all that you can do every day and more than fill your present space. At a daily minimum, you want to accomplish your *three* *most important tasks* (TMIT), and at a daily maximum you typically would not do more than your *six most important tasks* (SMIT). Typically, accomplishing your daily TMIT/SMIT enables you to Manifest your goal if you are doing all of your rituals properly by ensuring that you are performing efficient action. As you get more in tune with your ritual and in harmony with your Subconscious Mind, you will just *know* what they are when you perform your evening preview for your next day. Typically, performing your top three tasks will be enough to produce phenomenal results.

Emotion: One of P. J.'s Manifest Recipe's Fifteen (15) Key Ingredients to *Manifest Anything You Can Imagine.* Emotion is one of your two necessary elements, along with your burning-desire, that provide energy and propel your goal forward after you have created your thought-form. It is the fuel that moves everything. With your thought, you can create the greatest and potentially fastest Italian sports car ever made. But with no fuel, it can never and will never move. It is the energy that drives creation by feeling the desired outcome as already done, and it helps to merge your thoughts and actions with the Universal Laws.

Faith: One of P. J.'s Manifest Recipe's Fifteen (15) Key Ingredients to *Manifest Anything You Can Imagine.* Faith is one of your two initial building blocks along with Belief. You must have Faith that your Spirit, Spiritual DNA, and Spiritual Spark are Perfect. Universal Intelligence wants you to co-create with It, and It has structured Its Universal Laws to help you in every way possible. You possess within yourself right now all of the tools necessary to Manifest your goal, dreams, wishes, and Best-Life, and remember, you are an Eternal Spiritual Being having a limited physical experience. Faith is the confident expectation in the Manifestation of your want and burning-desire goal through the power of your thought.

Free Will: One of the most powerful abilities given to you by Universal Intelligence. One hundred percent trust has been placed in you to allow you to make any decision, good or bad, that you so desire. Use this superpower wisely.

Frequency: All of your thoughts are on frequencies, and they are all connected. This is how you communicate with others and the entire Universe. It is your vibrational energy that is emitted by your thoughts and emotions, and it determines what you attract to yourself.

Goal: One of P. J.'s Manifest Recipe's Fifteen (15) Key Ingredients to *Manifest Anything You Can Imagine*. Your goal is your highest and most emotion-filled *want*. It is your #1 desired outcome that you place 100 percent focus on when you *Manifest Anything You Can Imagine*. Your goal is what you desire with a *burning-desire* more than anything else. It is what you automatically think about when you are barely awake and roll over in bed at 3 a.m. I always want my *faith goal* so bad and with so much passion that *I can taste it*. The sum of all of your goals makes up the whole of your vision. I often refer to your *faith goal* as your *10x goal*.

Goal Coin ("VEGA Coin"): Your Visualization, Emotion, Goal, and Action P. J. MindsetCoach VEGA Coin that you keep in your pocket all day every day. Every time you touch or think about your P. J. MindsetCoach VEGA Coin, you will visualize a consistent picture on the screen of your mind with emotion motivating you to take action to meet your goal, grab it, embrace it, and enjoy it.

Goals: My three types: (1) *know*, (2) *think*, and (3) *Faith*. Your *know* goal is one you know you can accomplish. Your *think* goal is one you think you can accomplish. Your most important goal, and the only one I focus my coaching on with you, is your *Faith* goal. Your Faith goal is one you have absolutely no idea how you will accomplish. And that is what we need for you to *Manifest Anything You Can Imagine*. It must be based on 100 percent Faith, and a 100 percent *inside-out* approach based on a Belief and Faith mindset. An example of a Faith/10x goal would be me working with you and coaching you to turn your *annual* income into your *monthly* income.

Grab Your Goal: Toward the completion of your Manifesting process, you will need to step forward and *grab* your goal as it nears you. This is not the time to be timid or allow your paradigm to subvert all of your efforts. Oftentimes, for various reasons, people will flinch when their goal is about to be upon them and lose or delay the wonderful success they could have enjoyed. Have the Belief, Faith, and confidence that you are truly worthy of living and enjoying your Best-Life and taking action and accepting your Manifested goal when it is about to be delivered to you. Grab it, embrace it, enjoy it, love it, and live your Best-Life.

Gratitude: One of P. J.'s Manifest Recipe's Fifteen (15) Key Ingredients to *Manifest Anything You Can Imagine*. One of the most important elements and variables that will determine your happiness and success in Manifesting what you want. Every thought and action has an equal reaction in our world and Universe, and the level of Gratitude you express helps pull your goal toward you. It is your feeling of appreciation as if your goal is already present in your hands, which attracts more blessings to your life. Every action has an equal and opposite reaction. The emotion and energy you release when you are Grateful will return back to you more of what you are Grateful for. Be as Grateful and appreciative as if you have already received your goal and are living with it and enjoying it. By cultivating a mindset of Gratitude, you can shift your focus toward the positive aspects of your life, which in turn attracts more positive experiences toward you.

Higher-Faculties: "WIP RIM"—will, imagination, perception, reason, intuition, and memory. The higher-faculties given only to you and other human beings that set you apart from everything else on earth and in the animal kingdom. The key tools that enable you to Manifest. Identify which ones are your strongest ones and really work them. Think of them as *muscles* that you can make stronger with repetition and practice, and ideally turn each of them into a habit of yours. If you work them, they will improve. There is no such thing as a *bad* or *weak* WIP RIM higher-faculty.

I AM: A confident acknowledgment to the Universe that you are *One* with Universal Intelligence and the Universal Subconscious Mind. Always start every one of your Affirmations with "I AM So Happy and Grateful Now That…" This is the most powerful affirmation available to you to claim your identity as a divine being and to empower and energize you to *Manifest Anything You Can Imagine*.

Imagination: One of P. J.'s Manifest Recipe's Fifteen (15) Key Ingredients to *Manifest Anything You Can Imagine*. Also, it is one of your six (WIP RIM) will, imagination, perception, reason, intuition, and memory, higher-faculties that only you and other human beings possess. For me personally, imagination is one of my strongest higher-faculties along with my intuition. No other form of life that we know of has these higher-faculties. It is arguably the genesis and first step to _Manifest Anything_ *You Can Imagine*. Think of it as a *muscle* that you can make stronger with repetition and practice and ideally turn into a habit of yours. Your imagination creates your thoughts and your thoughts create your thought-form. Use it to build the image of whatever goal you want to achieve. Your imagination gives shape, form, and action to your *desires* in your Subconscious Mind. Imagination is where *everything* is created, in your thoughts and ideas. Everything in our world is created twice; first in our imagination in our mind and then with the physical-back of it in our material world, which we acquire through our actions. Everything around us and in our lives was first created in someone's imagination.

Impression of Increase: In order to be in alignment with Universal Intelligence and the Universal Subconscious Mind and to Manifest successfully, you must provide to every brother and sister with whom you interact a Use Value that is greater than the Cash Value they deliver to you. You should do this mentally as well as physically. Conquering this takes you to superstar status. Always deliver your impression of increase and have your fellow brothers and sisters look at you as an advancing person.

Intuition: *The sixth sense*, which for me personally is one of my strongest higher-faculties along with my imagination. My intuition is highly developed and yours can be too. Your intuition enables you to plug directly into Universal Intelligence and the Universal Subconscious Mind. It also allows you to read and process other people's energy and vibrations along with receiving a perfect answer from Universal Intelligence to every question and challenge you have. It is especially important in guiding you to make the best correct decisions. It is one of your six (WIP RIM) will, imagination, perception, reason, intuition, and memory higher-faculties that only you and other human beings possess. No other form of life that we know of has these higher-faculties. Think of it as a *muscle* that you can make stronger with repetition and practice and ideally turn into a habit of yours.

Law of Attraction: "Like attracts like." Technically, the Law of Vibration is a Primary Law and the Law of Attraction is a Secondary Law. The Law of Attraction is the principle that your thoughts and Beliefs create your reality, and you can Manifest your desires by focusing on positive and aligned thoughts and actions. It is the key to *Manifest Anything You Can Imagine* and to achieving your goal, dreams, and wishes.

Manifest: To co-create with Universal Intelligence and the Universal Subconscious Mind. The result of my *recipe* to create and live your Best-Life. To create through your Belief and Faith in alignment with Universal Laws and make real. Refers to the process of bringing into physical reality your desired experiences or conditions through aligning your thoughts, Beliefs, actions, and emotions with your desired outcome. This is a Holy Grail ability that you possess within you.

Meet Your Thought: As I detail in my book, your efficient actions meet your thought at *midfield* where you will Manifest your goal, grab it, celebrate it, and enjoy it. Meeting your thought halfway means aligning your actions and Beliefs with your desired outcomes and allowing Universal Intelligence to co-create with you in Manifesting your goal.

Memory: Your memory is one of your six (WIP RIM) will, imagination, perception, reason, intuition, and memory higher-faculties that only you and other human beings possess. No other form of life that we know of has these higher-faculties. Think of it as a *muscle* that you can make stronger with repetition and practice and ideally turn into a habit of yours.

Metaphysics: Metaphysics is a branch of philosophy that deals with questions about the nature of reality, existence, and the Universe. It explores fundamental concepts such as being, time, space, causality, mind, and substance. Metaphysics is concerned with understanding the fundamental nature of reality beyond what is observable through empirical evidence, and it often involves discussions about the nature of reality and existence. It can be divided into various subfields, such as cosmology, and it has been a central topic of philosophical inquiry for centuries.

Methods of Manifesting: The concept that "a lot of people Manifest differently" was shared with me by Bob Proctor. I provide you with my successful *recipe* with all of my Fifteen (15) Key Ingredients for you to *Manifest Anything You Can Imagine*. After you succeed at Manifesting, you can customize my recipe to your own unique strengths, abilities, and ideal process.

Mind: Your mind consists of your Conscious Mind, Subconscious Mind, and your Body. Your body is an instrument of your Mind. Dr. Thurman Fleet rediscovered this information in 1934, and it was and remains a major breakthrough that has benefited you and I beyond words. I consider it to be the most informative and beneficial image I have experienced in my life. Because of this, my next two books, tentatively titled *P. J.'s Mind* and *P. J.'s Magic Lamp*, are dedicated to further explaining your mind and how to use it in the best manner possible to *Manifest Anything You Can Imagine*. When most people are asked what their mind is, they respond that their mind is their *brain*. Your *brain* is no more your mind than your nose or toes are.

New Thought: A Spiritual centric movement that emphasizes the power of thought to shape your life and create your reality. It holds that you can transform your life by changing your thinking patterns and aligning yourself with the Universal Laws and principles, such as the Law of Oneness, the Law of Vibration, the Law of Attraction, the Law of Perpetual Increase, and the Law of Cause and Effect/ Law of Karma. As summarized by Thomas Troward, it is a philoso- phy that emphasizes the power of our thoughts and Beliefs to shape our reality and our ability to co-create with Universal Intelligence and the Universal Subconscious Mind.

New Thought "New School": P. J. DiNuzzo, Oprah Winfrey, Lady Gaga, Steve Harvey, Ariana Grande, Tray Rush, Keshia Rush, Beyoncé, Jay-Z, Will Smith, Esther Hicks, Jack Canfield, Rhonda Byrne, Walt Disney, Alesha Dixon, Maya Angelou, Jim Carrey, and Arnold Schwarzenegger.

New Thought "Old School": Most Asian philosophies, and those of Plato, William Shakespeare, Isaac Newton, Ludwig van Beethoven, James Allen, Abraham Lincoln, Ralph Waldo Emerson, Wallace Wattles, Thomas Troward, Andrew Carnegie, Thomas Edison, Albert Einstein, Napoleon Hill, Neville Goddard, U. S. Andersen, Earl Nightingale, and Bob Proctor.

P. J.'s Daily 5 a.m. Ritual: Good Morning... Good Day... Win Your Morning... Win Your Day... Own Your Morning... Own Your Day.

P. J.'s Daily Handwritten "Faith Goal" Ritual: Write out my "Faith Goal" Affirmation (I AM So Happy and Grateful Now That...) Fifty Times Per Day.

P. J.'s Fifteen (15) Key Ingredient Manifest Recipe to *Manifest Anything* You Can Imagine: BELIEF, FAITH, PURPOSE, THOUGHT, IMAGINATION, WANT, VISION, GOAL, BURNING-DESIRE, VISUALIZATION, EMOTION, ACTION, ACCEPTANCE, BUOYANCY, and GRATITUDE.

P. J.'s Magic Lamp: My "Magic Lamp" resides in my Subconscious Mind. Unlike Aladdin's Lamp that was limited to Three Wishes, my magic lamp grants me *unlimited* wishes and acts on *every* suggestion, I or others make. You have your own special unlimited magic lamp that you can relate to inside of your Subconscious Mind that is ready, willing, and able to start to *Manifest Anything You Can Imagine* and deliver your goal, dreams, and wishes to you today.

P. J.'s Mind: My Conscious Mind, my Subconscious Mind, and my Body all working together seamlessly in harmony to *Manifest Anything You Can Imagine.* You and I live simultaneously on three planes: Conscious Mind, Subconscious Mind, and body. My body is an instrument of my mind. The concept for my next book, tentatively titled *P. J.'s Mind*, explains my Mind, and yours, in fascinating detail. The image of our *mind*, rediscovered by Dr. Thurman Fleet in 1934, is the most important, informative, and inspirational image I have ever witnessed, studied, and understood in my life.

P. J.'s **"Purpose"**: Delivering peace of mind and inspiration to my fellow brothers and sisters, especially women and children in need, and most especially women and children of color who are in need, through food, clothing, shelter, healthcare, transportation, education, and most importantly, Spirituality and Faith. I deliver this peace of mind and inspiration to my fellow brothers and sisters, especially women and children in need, and most especially women and children of color who are in need, through my biological family, my team family, my family of clients, my community family, and my Spiritual family... every single fellow brother and sister of mine on this planet.

P. J.'s **Weekly Rituals:** Sunday evening's Week Preview, P. J.'s Daily 5 a.m. Ritual; goal affirmation, Gratitude, Belief, Faith, purpose, forgiveness, declaration, self-confidence formula, visualization, spaced-repetition (goal affirmation and visualization) throughout the day, VEGA Coin throughout the day, evening review and preview. Handwrite my "Faith goal" fifty times every day.

Paradigm: A set of Beliefs and values that others and you have *programmed* into your Subconscious Mind since the day you were born. Your paradigm was programmed 100 percent by other people until you were approximately age six through their suggestions. I work with you to reprogram these thousands of suggestions during the first six years of your life you were unable to reject or cancel because your Conscious Mind was not yet developed. Whether you succeed at Manifesting depends upon your ability to be in control of your paradigm. *Cancel* or *reject every* improper or negative suggestion made to your Subconscious Mind/Paradigm. It will either make or break all of your efforts to *Manifest Anything You Can Imagine.*

Perception: As Wayne Dyer stated, "If you change the way you look at things, the things you look at change." Think of the perception a billionaire would have of a financial challenge you think you are experiencing. Have the perception of them as someone who is financially savvy and you may find a solution to your financial challenge immediately, and it would vanish and disappear. It is one of your six (WIP RIM) will, imagination, perception, reason, intuition, and memory higher-faculties that only you and other human beings possess. No other form of life that we know of has these higher-faculties. Think of it as a *muscle* that you can make stronger with repetition and practice and ideally turn into a habit of yours. Shift your perception and you change and improve everything. Look at it from a different seat or angle or another person's point of view, with an open mind, and watch your problems wash away.

Perpetual Increase of Life: The key Universal Law that is the basis for continuous expression, expansion, increase, growth, and happiness. Universal Intelligence created our Universe and the world you and I live in under the Law of Perpetual Increase to further express, expand, increase, and grow. The Law of Perpetual Increase states that everything in the Universe is constantly expanding and increasing, and that you can tap into this abundance through your positive thoughts, Faith, Belief, and Gratitude. This Law applies to all aspects of your life, including your physical, mental, financial, emotional, and Spiritual growth. According to this law, you should strive to continuously improve yourself in order to align with the natural expansion of the Universe. By embracing this law, you can experience greater abundance, success, and fulfillment and live your Best-Life.

Physical-Back (of your Goal): After you have created the front of your goal with your thought and thought-form, you finish your work with efficient action to materialize the physical-back of your goal and grab it, embrace it, and enjoy it. This process is complemented throughout by all Fifteen (15) Key Ingredients in "P. J.'s Manifesting Recipe."

Purpose: One of P. J.'s Manifest Recipe's Fifteen (15) Key Ingredients to *Manifest Anything* You Can Imagine. Your *why* in your life. Why you are here on earth. The two most important days of your life are the day you were born and the day you figured out and understood the reason *why*. It will take a while to figure out, but once you do, you will never be the same. Your purpose is one of the primary and key elements in your process of Manifesting your goal. It often will be the last ingredient you will define and be comfortable with that you got correct and to your liking when you begin to learn how to *Manifest Anything* You Can Imagine. My purpose—my *why*—is to deliver peace of mind and inspiration to my fellow brothers and sisters, especially women and children in need, and most especially women and children of color who are in need, through food, clothing, shelter, healthcare, transportation, education, and, most importantly, Spirituality and Faith. I deliver this peace of mind and inspiration to my fellow brothers and sisters, especially women and children in need, and most especially women and children of color who are in need through my biological family, my team family, my family of clients, my community family, and my Spiritual family... each and every one of my fellow brothers and sisters on earth.

Reason: It is your #1 tool for you to use to protect your Subconscious Mind and paradigm. It gives you the ability to think. It is your *reason* that you apply with your Conscious Mind to *reject* or *cancel* any negative suggestions before they enter your Subconscious Mind and take hold. It is one of your six (WIP RIM) will, imagination, perception, reason, intuition, and memory higher-faculties that to the best of our knowledge only you and other human beings possess. No other form of life has these higher-faculties. Think of it as a *muscle* that you can make stronger with repetition and practice and ideally turn into a habit of yours.

Repetition: Repetition is one of your mandatory "daily building blocks" necessary to *Manifest Anything You Can Imagine*. Without consistent and disciplined repetition, you are not going to get very far with your success in Manifesting because you will not be able to win over your paradigm. Additionally, you will not be able to "reprogram" your Subconscious Mind/Paradigm as you desire, and you will not be able to maintain your high-vibration and buoyancy. There is no substitute for it on your road to success. Think of it as another *muscle* that you can make stronger with practice and ideally turn into a habit of yours. Repetition positions you for success by acting as one of the best *habits* you can possibly acquire. Some great examples to apply the benefits of repetition to in your daily ritual are Goal Coin ("VEGA Coin"), P. J.'s Daily 5 a.m. Ritual, P. J.'s Daily Handwritten "Faith Goal" Ritual, and P. J.'s Manifest Recipe's Fifteen (15) Key Ingredients to *Manifest Anything You Can Imagine*: BELIEF, FAITH, PURPOSE, THOUGHT, IMAGINATION, WANT, VISION, GOAL, BURNING-DESIRE, VISUALIZA-TION, EMOTION, ACTION, ACCEPTANCE, BUOYANCY, and GRATITUDE.

SMIT (Six Most Important Tasks): In order for you to *Manifest Anything You Can Imagine*, you must more than fill your present space by performing action, specifically efficient action. Your daily efficient action should be a minimum of your TMIT and a maximum of your SMIT. Once you are in harmony with your daily ritual, your Subconscious Mind will let you know what these actions are. It will be obvious to you what your most important tasks are that you get to do each day when you perform your "evening preview" the night before. Your six most important (daily) tasks are the actions that will make the biggest impact toward your goals and your Best-Life and require your focus, discipline, and effort.

Spaced-Repetition: Every two or three hours from 8 a.m. to 5 p.m. verbally perform your "Faith Goal" affirmation for two minutes with emotion and then visualize for two minutes with emotion ideally in front of your bathroom mirror to enhance your message to Universal Intelligence and the Universal Subconscious Mind. Systematically repeating your affirmation and visualization throughout your day helps you to maintain your buoyancy, high-vibration, and focus and keeps you in harmony to *Manifest Anything You Can Imagine*.

Spirit: This is one of the most important elements for your self-confidence as you need to know in your heart of hearts that your Spirit is made in the exact likeness of Universal Intelligence and the Universal Subconscious Mind. Your Spirit, Spiritual Spark, and Spiritual DNA are perfect and provide you with all the ability you will ever need from Universal Intelligence to *Manifest Anything You Can Imagine*. Knowing that you have Perfect Spirit, Perfect Spiritual DNA, and Perfect Spiritual Spark allows you to have confidence that you can accomplish anything you desire, working in harmony with Universal Intelligence and the Universal Subconscious Mind in accordance with Its Universal Laws. It is Universal Intelligence's energy and power that permeate all things and connect you directly to the Divine and the Universal Subconscious Mind. It is the source of your co-creative power and enables you to Manifest your Best-Life.

Spiritual DNA: This is one of the most important elements for your self-confidence as you need to know in your heart of hearts that your Spiritual DNA is made in the exact likeness of Universal Intelligence and the Universal Subconscious Mind. This is one of the most important elements for your self-confidence as your Spiritual DNA is perfect right down to the smallest amount of matter within you. Your Spirit, Spiritual Spark, and Spiritual DNA are perfect and provide you with all the ability you will ever need from Universal Intelligence to *Manifest Anything You Can Imagine*. Knowing that you have Perfect Spirit, Perfect Spiritual DNA, and Perfect Spiritual Spark allows you to have confidence that you can accomplish anything that you desire, working in harmony with Universal Intelligence and the Universal Subconscious Mind in accordance with Its the Universal Laws. It is Universal Intelligence's energy and power that permeate all things and connect you directly to the Divine and the Universal Subconscious Mind. It is the source of your co-creative power and enables you to Manifest your Best-Life.

Spiritual Spark: This is one of the most important elements for your self-confidence as you need to know in your heart of hearts that your Spiritual Spark is made in the exact likeness of Universal Intelligence and the Universal Subconscious Mind. This is one of the most important elements for your self-confidence as one initial Spark from your Spirit can start a brush fire or wild fire of amazing events for you and enable you to *Manifest Anything You Can Imagine*. Your Spirit, Spiritual Spark, and Spiritual DNA are perfect and provide you with all the ability you will ever need from Universal Intelligence. Knowing that you have Perfect Spirit, Perfect Spiritual DNA, and Perfect Spiritual Spark allows you to have confidence that you can accomplish anything that you desire, working in harmony with Universal Intelligence and the Universal Subconscious Mind in accordance with Its Universal Laws. It is Universal Intelligence's energy and power that permeate all things and connect you directly to the Divine and the Universal Subconscious Mind. It is the source of your co-creative power and enables you to Manifest your Best-Life.

Starting: As a rule, it is best to start to *Manifest Anything You Can Imagine* in your current job, career, or business and not wait. It works best for you to start from the place right where you are at today.

Subconscious Mind: Your Subconscious Mind is one of the three major elements, along with your Conscious Mind and your body, that make up what I refer to as your mind. When most people are asked what their mind is, they respond that their mind is their *brain*. Your brain is no more your mind than your nose or toes are. Your Subconscious Mind is your *subjective mind*, which deals with, reacts to, and relates to emotion. It is your emotional mind, and in order to communicate with it, you must do it with emotion or it will not *hear* you at all. Your higher-faculties (WIP RIM) allow you to access the genius within you and your Subconscious Mind. Your Subconscious Mind is your subjective and emotion-driven mind directly connected to the Universal Subconscious Mind. Your Subconscious Mind is your *treasury* where your desire will initiate and grow into a burning-desire for you to *Manifest Anything You Can Imagine*. It is your Intuitive Subconscious Mind that separates you from all other life on earth, and your higher-faculties that allow you to access the genius within yourself. Your Conscious Mind is very powerful. Think of its energy and power as a computer processing chip the size of your fist vs. your Subconscious Mind, which has the energy and power of a computer processing chip the size of an entire football field... stacked all the way up into and beyond the clouds above you.

Success/Successful: As defined by Earl Nightingale, success is the progressive realization of a worthy ideal and goal. According to Nightingale, success is not simply a matter of achieving wealth or status, but rather it is the ongoing process of moving toward a meaningful objective. He believed that success requires a clear sense of purpose, a positive attitude, and consistent action toward a goal that is aligned with one's values and desires. Nightingale emphasized the importance of setting specific, measurable, and achievable goals and working toward them with focus, discipline, and perseverance. He Believed that success is not a destination, but rather a journey, and that anyone can achieve it with the right mindset and effort. Never forget that success with regard to progressive realization of your worthy ideal regarding health, wealth, happiness, companionship, or your Best-Life goal is 5 percent strategy and 95 percent mindset.

Suggestions: Suggestions are arguably the most powerful force on earth and in the Universe. A suggestion is the *mustard seed* starting point from which every goal that you achieve originates and grows. You have a "magic lamp" inside of you within your Subconscious Mind that takes immediate action on *any* suggestion that you or any other person, entity, or format make into it. Your Subconscious Mind is trusting you to protect it and assumes that any suggestion given to it from someone or something else meets with your approval and that you want to Manifest it.

The Secret: The Secret is the Law of Attraction, which empowers you to _Manifest Anything You Can Imagine._ You have All Power of All Time within you working hand in hand with Universal Intelligence and the Universal Subconscious Mind to co-create your goal and live your Best-Life.

Thought: One of P. J.'s Manifest Recipe's Fifteen (15) Key Ingredients to _Manifest Anything You Can Imagine._ Thought is the original creation point of all that you Manifest. Your thoughts and thought-form on the screen of your mind create everything in your Life. Your thoughts are on frequencies that are all connected to each other. It is your thought that initiates the Manifesting process and allows you to _Manifest Anything You Can Imagine_ by beginning to move all available and appropriate resources into the creation and development of your goal.

Thought Universe: You live in a "Thought World" within a perfect and Infinite "Thought Universe" all created by Universal Intelligence and the Universal Subconscious Mind. Everything on earth is first created in your and others thought and then materializes under the Universal Laws in our Thought Universe.

Thought World: You live in a "Thought World" within a Perfect and Infinite "Thought Universe" all created by Universal Intelligence and the Universal Subconscious Mind. Everything on earth is first created in your and others thought and then materializes under the Universal Laws in our Thought Universe.

TMIT (Three Most Important Tasks): In order for you to _Manifest Anything_ *You Can Imagine,* you must more than fill your present space by performing action, specifically efficient action. Your daily efficient action should be a minimum of your TMIT and a maximum of your SMIT. Once you are in harmony with your daily ritual, your Subconscious Mind will let you know what these actions are. It will be obvious to you what your most important tasks are that you get to do each day when you perform your "evening preview" the night before. Your three most important (daily) tasks are the actions that will make the biggest impact toward your goals and your Best-Life and require your focus, discipline, and effort.

Two Most Important Days of Your Life: The day you were born and the day you figured out and understood the reason *why.*

Universal Intelligence: The Original, Perfect, Infinite, and Universal Supreme Power. It is a Thinking Power that is literally *everywhere* and always has your best interests at heart. It is the Infinite Intelligence and Wisdom of the Universe, which is accessible to all through the power of the mind. The Supreme Power, Creator, and Originator of All. The One. I AM. Divine Oneness. The Ultimate Infinite Supreme Perfect Power. The Infinite and Divine Wisdom that permeates all things and guides us toward our highest potential and purpose in Life.

Universal Intelligence Original Thinking Substance: There is a Universal Intelligent Original Thinking Substance from which all things are made, and which, in Its original state, permeates, penetrates, and fills the interspaces of the entire Universe. Your thought in this Substance produces the thought-form and thing that you image by your thought. You can form things in your thought, and by impressing your thought-form upon Universal Intelligent Thinking Substance, you can cause the thing you think about to be created.

Universal Intelligence Science (or Universal Science): All of the Universal Laws working in harmony that govern the entire Universe such as the metaphysical Law of Attraction. The Science of Universal Intelligence and the Universal Subconscious Mind, which is an exact science based on Universal Law(s). Since it is an exact science, you can confidently live in harmony with it to *Manifest Anything You Can Imagine.* You and I live in a perfect thought world within a Perfect and Infinite Thought Universe all guided by the science of Its Universal Laws.

Universal Laws: The fundamental principles established by Universal Intelligence that govern our entire Perfect and Infinite Universe, made up of the Universal Laws, including, but not limited to, the Laws of (1) Divine Oneness, (2) Vibration, (3) Attraction, (4) Cause and Effect/Karma, (5) Gratitude, (6) Assumption, (7) Compensation, (8) Polarity, (9) Inspired Action, (10) Correspondence, (11) Perpetual Transmutation of Energy, (12) Relativity, (13) Rhythm, (14) Gender, (15) Perpetual Increase & Motion, (16) Giving and Receiving, (17) Increase of Life, and (18) Wealth. The Universal Laws are the principles that govern the functioning of the Universe and influence all aspects of your life and all life. These laws are seen as immutable and impartial, meaning they apply to everyone and everything equally, regardless of personal beliefs or circumstances. Two of the most commonly recognized Universal Laws include the Law of Attraction, which states that like attracts like and that one's thoughts and emotions can influence their reality, and the Law of Cause and Effect/Law of Karma, which states that every action has a corresponding reaction or consequence. By understanding and living in harmony with these laws, you can tap into the natural flow and energy of the Universe to *Manifest Anything You Can Imagine*.

Universal Subconscious Mind: The Supreme Universal Intelligence and Subconscious Mind that rules the entire Universe that we are *all connected to* and is inside of you and me. It contains All knowledge of All time. The Universal Subconscious Mind is the Infinite Intelligence and Creative Force of the Universe that responds to our thoughts and beliefs to co-create our goal with us to *Manifest Anything You Can Imagine*. The Universal Subconscious Mind is the Infinite and all-encompassing field of consciousness that permeates everything and is the source of all creation and Manifestation.

Universal Way: Your desired way of living your life, every day, from *inside-out* rather than *outside-in*—living your life according to how Universal Intelligence created our Perfect and Infinite Universe for you with Its flawless Universal Laws. By properly following these Universal Laws by acting in harmony with the Universal Way, you create your goal and *Manifest Anything You Can Imagine* and enjoy your Best-Life.

VEGA "Goal" Coin: Your Visualization, Emotion, Goal, and Action "Coin" that you keep in your pocket all day every day. Every time you touch or think about your P. J. MindsetCoach™ VEGA Coin, you will visualize a consistent picture on the screen of your mind with emotion, motivating you to take action to meet your goal, grab it, embrace it, and enjoy it.

Vibration: The Law of Attraction starts with the Law of Vibration. Technically, the Law of Vibration is a primary Law and the Law of Attraction is a secondary Law. Your vibration starts in your own mind as your vibration is generated by your mind. You are a mass of infinitely powerful energy and you function on frequencies. Everything on earth emits energy and vibrates. Energy functions on frequencies that are a level of Vibration. There are an infinite number of Vibrations and Frequencies. Feelings in your Subconscious Mind are your conscious awareness of your vibration as well as other people's vibrations.

Vision: One of P. J.'s Manifest Recipe's Fifteen (15) Key Ingredients to *Manifest Anything You Can Imagine*. I AM So Happy and Grateful Now That I understand that my goals, which comprise the whole of my vision, are primarily for growth, not achievement. The sum of all of your goals makes up the whole of your vision. Think of your vision as large letter "V" from the front of your forehead looking outward. Think of round circles or balls in this letter V that have the names of your different goals marked on each separate ball. Your outward looking vision contains all of your important goals. To Manifest your "Faith 10x" goal, you choose and focus on the *one* most important goal within your vision.

Vision Board: A fun tool to help maintain your emotional involvement, high-vibration, and buoyancy throughout your day to *Manifest Anything You Can Imagine*. For example, let us imagine that your 10x "Faith Goal" is a new car. You would cut out attractive pictures of your car, including many different angles and features, and tape or glue them to your vision board. Keep your vision board in a location where you can easily see it throughout your day or your evening. Every time you look at your vision board, visualize yourself in it, enjoying your new car every way possible. Additionally, every time you look at your vision board, do so with emotion and a high-vibration.

Visualization: One of P. J.'s Manifest Recipe's Fifteen (15) Key Ingredients to *Manifest Anything You Can Imagine*. For me, visualization is at least in a tie for my #1 most powerful *ingredient* that I use to Manifest. I AM very good at visualization and get deeply and emotionally involved. Too much stress cannot be laid on the importance of your imagination and frequent visualization of your goal and mental image. Your visualization, emotion, goal, and action P.J. MindsetCoach VEGA Coin should be kept in your pocket all day every day. Every time you touch or think about your VEGA Coin, you will visualize a consistent picture on the screen of your mind of your 10x "Faith Goal," with emotion motivating you to take action to meet your goal and grab it. Visualization is a key element of your spaced-repetition (goal affirmation and visualization) throughout your day. Systematically repeating your affirmation and visualization throughout your day helps you to maintain your buoyancy and focus and keeps you in harmony so you can *Manifest Anything You Can Imagine*.

Want: One of P. J.'s Manifest Recipe's Fifteen (15) Key Ingredients to *Manifest Anything You Can Imagine*. When I AM starting to coach anyone, the first thing I ask them is "what do you want?" Because you have to know what you want before you can even begin to get to the *starting point* of Manifesting your goal. Your want should be something you truly want more than anything else on earth. I AM so deeply invested in my want that I can "taste" it. When I roll over in bed in the middle of the night it is right at the front of my mind. Once you have identified your want and you focus your thoughts on it enough, you will push it down into and deposit it into the *treasury* of your Subconscious Mind. It is the first "switch" that must be properly flipped to *Manifest Anything You Can Imagine*.

Will: Persistence. Without a strong will and persistence, you are not going to get very far with your success in Manifesting. It is one of your six (WIP RIM) will, imagination, perception, reason, intuition, and memory higher-faculties that to the best of our knowledge only you and other human beings possess. No other form of life has these higher-faculties. There is no substitute for it in your desire to succeed. Think of it as a *muscle* that you can make stronger with repetition and practice and ideally turn into a habit of yours. In order to *Manifest Anything You Can Imagine,* you must be disciplined and pass the *will and persistence test.* You are going to be tested, and persevering through your challenges will deliver the goal of your dreams and wishes. Will allows you to succeed by staying focused and maintaining your discipline. The average person's concentration lasts for only seconds. Focus increases the amplitude of the power flowing into us, increasing our energy and enhancing our success.

WIP RIM: See *Higher-Faculties.*

About P. J. DiNuzzo

"It feels so good inside that we are starting a lifelong success-filled journey together. Take the leap. Jump on board with me. And hitch a ride, the greatest ride of your life."
—P. J. DiNuzzo

P. J. DiNuzzo is the Founder, President, Lead Consultant, Chief Investment Officer (CIO), and Chief Compliance Officer (CCO) for DiNuzzo Private Wealth, Inc., DiNuzzo Middle-Market Family Office™, and DiNuzzo Tax and Wealth Management, which has operated as an SEC Registered Investment Advisory Firm since 1989 and currently manages $899 million in assets under management as of June 30, 2023. P. J. is also President and Founder of P.

J. MindsetCoach™ and DiNuzzo Real Estate. P. J. has devoted his entire professional career to tax planning, wealth planning, investment planning, risk management planning, client service, and investment implementation. He was approved as one of the first one hundred advisors in the United States with SMA, ETF, and Mutual Fund Institutional Manager, Dimensional Fund Advisors (DFA) in the early 1990s. DiNuzzo Private Wealth, Inc./DiNuzzo Middle-Market Family Office/DiNuzzo Wealth Management was one of the first few hundred fee-only firms in the US in the late 1980s and has been consistently ranked as one of the top five hundred firms in the country by *Financial Advisor* magazine. Under P. J.'s leadership, DiNuzzo Private Wealth, Inc./DiNuzzo Family Office/DiNuzzo Wealth Management, on numerous occasions, has been recognized as one of the "Best Places to Work" and was awarded the honor of "#1 Best Place to Work" in Western Pennsylvania/Pittsburgh in 2008, 2013, and 2016 by the *Pittsburgh Business Times*. Additionally, P. J. has been awarded the prestigious multiyear designation as a Five Star Wealth Manager. The award is given to Wealth Managers in Pittsburgh and across the US who satisfy key client criteria and score the highest in overall client satisfaction.

P. J. has earned the distinguished Personal Financial Specialist (PFS™) designation. The American Institute of Certified Public Accountants (AICPA), a national professional organization of CPA professionals, grants the PFS credential only to certified public accountants with a significant personal financial planning education and experience. Candidates must meet six necessary requirements including an arduous technical exam and a peer review of their ability to demonstrate significant experience in a wide range of comprehensive personal financial planning disciplines.

P. J. has also written a half dozen books, including the *Wall Street Journal* and *USA Today* bestselling book *The DiNuzzo "Middle-Market Family Office™" Breakthrough: Creating Strategic Tax, Risk, Cash-Flow, and*

Lifestyle Options for Successful Privately-Held Business Owners and Affluent Families, Don't Get Killed on Taxes: 20 of the Most Common Reasons You're Sending Too Much Money to the IRS, The Seven Keys to Investing Success, The Secret to Scale: An Entrepreneur's Guide to Starting, Growing, and Exiting Your Business with Maximum Profit and Peace of Mind (a collaboration with several successful business consultants), and multiple additional books that are scheduled to release after this one.

P. J. also built a successful real estate company that owns and operates a real estate portfolio that generates substantial NNN (triple-net) rental income.

And P. J. also operates a successful Self-Improvement Success Coaching business, P. J. MindsetCoach™, as well as a Self-Improvement training company, P. J. MindsetCoach Institute™ where he helps high-potential people Manifest their dream lives no matter where they are in the world.

P. J. has been interviewed on numerous occasions regarding Middle-Market Family Offices, Closely Held Businesses, High-Net-Worth Individuals, Strategic Asset Allocation, Portfolio Diversification, Indexing, Rebalancing, and Retirement Income Planning on various television and radio programs including *Private Wealth* magazine with Russ Alan Prince, *Oprah & Friends* with Jean Chatzky on XM Radio, *Power Lunch* on CNBC, KDKA-TV2's *Sunday Business Page* with Jon Delano, ABC TV9 WCPO.com, and The Street.com TV.

P. J. has also been interviewed and quoted on a number of occasions regarding Strategic Asset Allocation, Portfolio Diversification, Indexing, Rebalancing, and Retirement Income Planning in various national, regional, and local magazines including *Kiplinger's Personal Finance* Retirement Planning, MarketWatch from Dow Jones, *Morningstar, SmartMoney, BusinessWeek, Investment Advisor, Financial Planning, NAPFA Advisor,* the *Wall Street Transcript, Wealth Management Exchange, Wealth Manager, Bottom Line Personal, InvestmentNews, Financial Advisor,* and IARFC's the *Register.*

He has also been interviewed and quoted on numerous occasions in various national, regional, and local newspapers and websites including the *Wall Street Journal*, *Barron's*, Reuters, Bankrate.com, CBS News, YAHOO! Finance, *Pittsburgh Post-Gazette*, U.S. News & World Report, MSN Money, *Chicago Sun-Times*, FT.com *Financial Times*, SmartMoneySelect.com, the *Atlanta Journal-Constitution*, *St. Louis Post-Dispatch*, Chicago Board Options Exchange, *Pittsburgh Business Times*, the *Sharon Herald*, the *Christian Science Monitor*, the *Beaver County Times*, *Pittsburgh Tribune-Review*, MutualFundWire.com, *Gulf News*, TMC.net, Comcast.net Finance, Rydex Investments, FreeRealTime.com, Individual.com, Lockheed Federal Credit Union, Invest n Retire, ABC TV9's WCPO.com, *Fort Worth Star-Telegram*, KYPost.com, Jim Prevor's *Perishable Pundit*, *Reading Eagle*, the *Toledo Blade*, Horsesmouth, DemocraticUnderground.com, the Community Investment Network, *Daily Herald*, Scripps News, the *Modesto Bee*, Hitched, Prime, *El Paso Times*, Paladin Advisor, Advisor Max, Denverpost.com, Oswego Daily News, The Dollar Stretcher, the *Ledger*, the *Columbus Dispatch*, *Savannah Morning News*, and Hampton Roads News Channel.

P. J. is also a sought-after speaker and self-improvement coach in the personal success, business success, and financial success sectors. Through his speaking and coaching, P. J. has helped thousands of people around the world achieve greater health, wealth, and happiness.

P. J. is a member of the Financial Planning Association (FPA), the American Institute of Certified Public Accountants (AICPA), the Pennsylvania Institute of Certified Public Accountants (PICPA), and the National Association of Tax Professionals (NATP).

P. J. chose football in lieu of a Major League Baseball offer from the Houston Astros to play with their Class A Team, as he attended and played football at Indiana University under Head Coach Lee Corso in the Big Ten (Bloomington, Indiana) and also at the University of Pittsburgh under Head Coach Jackie Sherrill. He later received his Bachelor of Science in Business Administration from Geneva College in Beaver Falls, PA. His graduate studies culminated in a Master of Business Administration (MBA) from the Katz Graduate School of Business at the University of Pittsburgh and a Master of Science in Tax Law (MSTx) from Robert Morris University at the downtown Pittsburgh campus. P. J. received his Certified Public Accountant (CPA) designation from the State of Delaware.

P. J. was a member of the Investment Committee on the Endowment Board for Valley Care Associates, a nonprofit organization providing adult day care, home safety consulting, and physical modifications for older people in Allegheny and Beaver Counties. He has served as a Finance Council Board Member for St. Blaise Church and is a member of the Department of Finance Advisory Board for Robert Morris University. He is a volunteer for and supports Habitat for Humanity and the Red Door Program for people experiencing homelessness, and he is committed to his churches in Midland and Pittsburgh's South Side. He has served on the Board of Directors for the Hope House and The Center, both of which are located in Midland, PA, and support the women and youth of the community. He is a lifelong resident of the Pittsburgh and Western Pennsylvania area. He devoted over twelve years to helping and assisting numerous young men in Pittsburgh's inner city and surrounding areas by supporting and coaching over one thousand basketball games at the Amateur Athletic Union (AAU), elementary, middle school, junior high, and high school levels, attempting to teach and instill in them teamwork, trust, structure, discipline, and hard work.

A free ebook edition is available with the purchase of this book.

To claim your free ebook edition:
1. Visit MorganJamesBOGO.com
2. Sign your name CLEARLY in the space
3. Complete the form and submit a photo of the entire copyright page
4. You or your friend can download the ebook to your preferred device

Morgan James
BOGO™

A **FREE** ebook edition is available for you or a friend with the purchase of this print book.

CLEARLY SIGN YOUR NAME ABOVE

Instructions to claim your free ebook edition:
1. Visit MorganJamesBOGO.com
2. Sign your name CLEARLY in the space above
3. Complete the form and submit a photo of this entire page
4. You or your friend can download the ebook to your preferred device

Print & Digital Together Forever.

Snap a photo   Free ebook   Read anywhere